SPEAKING UP

New Voices *on* War *and* Peace *in* Nova Scotia

Edited by **Maya Eichler, Reina Green,** *and* **Tracy Moniz**

Nimbus Publishing Limited
3660 Strawberry Hill Street, Halifax, NS, B3K 5A9
(902) 455-4286
nimbus.ca

Printed and bound in Canada
NB 1596

Editor: Raya P. Morrison
Design: Rudi Tusek
Cover: *Figurative Camo*, 16 x 20 inches, oil on canvas, 2019, by Jessica Lynn Wiebe
Quote on p. 175 from Gifford, C. G. "Pathfinder." In *This Was My War: A Collection of Memories of the 1939-1945 Conflict*, Little Daisy Press, 1992, used with permission.

Library and Archives Canada Cataloguing in Publication

Title: Speaking up : new voices on war and peace in Nova Scotia / edited by Maya Eichler, Reina Green, and Tracy Moniz.
Other titles: Speaking up (Nimbus Publishing)
Names: Eichler, Maya, 1974- editor. | Green, Reina, editor. | Moniz, Tracy, editor.
Identifiers: Canadiana (print) 20220266107 | Canadiana (ebook) 20220266581 | ISBN 9781774711255 (softcover) | ISBN 9781774711781 (EPUB)
Subjects: LCSH: Militarism—Nova Scotia—History. | LCSH: Nova Scotia—History, Military.
Classification: LCC FC2320.M5 S64 2022 | DDC 355.02/1309716—dc23

Nimbus Publishing acknowledges the financial support for its publishing activities from the Government of Canada, the Canada Council for the Arts, and from the Province of Nova Scotia. We are pleased to work in partnership with the Province of Nova Scotia to develop and promote our creative industries for the benefit of all Nova Scotians.

PRAISE FOR *SPEAKING UP*

We live in a community where we celebrate military history at the annual Nova Scotia International Tattoo but also champion the "dialogue across divides" work of the iconic Pugwash conferences to bring "insight and reason to bear on the catastrophic threat posed to humanity by nuclear and other weapons of mass destruction."

But *Speaking Up* explores more than those obvious divides. In this progressive Nova Scotian reimagining of the issues around war and peace, we learn the stories of soldiers who don't fit the norms of sex/gender, sexuality, race, or ethnicity. We hear voices from African Nova Scotian and Mi'kmaw communities whose stories of service and sacrifice have long been marginalized. And we explore art and war and remembrance.

Many of the voices in *Speaking Up* are new, previously unheard, but the editors have done an excellent job of connecting them with the more traditional narratives. Collectively, these voices and stories offer new patterns of understanding and challenge us to think differently about the vital issues of war and peace.

– Stephen Kimber, author of
Sailors, Slackers and Blind Pigs: Halifax at War

Speaking Up is an insightful anthology that explores Nova Scotia's complex relationship with the military. While Canadian military stories typically focus on an overseas battlefield, with soldiers, sailors, and aircrew fighting the enemy, *Speaking Up* instead relates the often-overlooked narratives of women, men, and LGBTQ2S+ peoples fighting against racism, sexism, colonialism, and homophobia in relation to the military.

These compelling stories—framed by accessible academic introductions—are ideal for educational contexts, particularly high school and undergraduate courses, drawing readers into the lives of military members, military families, refugees, peace activists, and artists. As a whole, the volume offers a nuanced and critical perspective that illuminates societal interconnections by blurring the binaries of military/civilian, friend/foe, national/international, war/peace, and patriotism/pacifism.

– Dr. Nancy Taber, Professor, Adult Education
Program Director, Brock University

Speaking Up: New Voices on War and Peace in Nova Scotia takes a critical lens to the military-industrial complex that permeates North America. With first-hand stories of people—from refugees to those in military service—the reader gets to peek behind the curtain to see a different perspective of war; one that goes beyond news tickers and Remembrance Day memorials. This book shows the human experience and consequences of a country and a province built on a foundation of colonialism and trimmed with patriotic rhetoric. *Speaking Up* is a challenging read but a must for everyone if we are to see the full scope of war and how it impacts our perceptions of society and people.

– Rebecca Thomas, Mi'kmaw author

Speaking Up is an engaging volume that broadens the focus of war and peace in a province and former colony with a long military presence. The edited collection encompasses an impressive breadth of experiences in both historical and contemporary contexts, told in a refreshing variety of formats.

...The revisited historiography of war and peace in Nova Scotia makes *Speaking Up* an important book for readers interested in Nova Scotia's long history of war and peace. Beyond this, the volume impressively demonstrates that an inclusive and decentred approach to the telling and sharing of history can be done exceptionally well, and as such could appeal to a much broader spectrum of readers interested in the craft of "doing history."

– Dr. Emily Burton, Oral Historian,
Canadian Museum of Immigration at Pier 21

To those who have shared their story,
to those whose story has yet to be told,
and to those whose story
will forever remain untold

Table of Contents

Introduction: Telling Stories of War and Peace in Nova Scotia

Maya Eichler, Reina Green, and Tracy Moniz

Canada is said to be a country shaped by war—mass mobilization during the two world wars was crucial to creating a pan-Canadian identity. The more-than decade-long military engagement in Afghanistan is seen to have brought back the idea of Canada as a warrior nation, a nation that holds its military in high regard. But Canada is also a country that has an ambivalent relationship to war. Preferring to see themselves as peacekeepers rather than warriors, Canadians have an at-times uneasy relationship with their military. That said, most Canadians are reluctant to embrace an outright anti-militarist stance.

As the impact of war on Canada continues to be debated, the military's role in shaping Nova Scotia's history and identity is rarely questioned. We attend military events such as Remembrance Day or the Royal Nova Scotia International Tattoo. We pass military memorials and bases without a second thought. The military is a key employer in the province; our economy is dependent on military industry, and many Nova Scotians have first-hand experience with the demands of military life, whether as a military member themselves or as a family member. Similarly, the stories told about Nova Scotian history tend to focus on narratives of war and militarism. Historical accounts mostly bring into view the experiences of male soldiers and their families during the two world wars. The dominant narrative of Nova Scotian history as military history is important but tells only part of the story.

What is lost in the taken-for-granted narrative of Nova Scotia's military history are the less-visible stories of war and peace: contemporary stories; stories told from outside the military community; stories of soldiers who don't fit the norms of sex, gender, sexuality, race, or ethnicity; and anti-militarist stories. This collection includes stories from the province's diverse communities, ranging from former members of the Canadian Armed Forces to members of the African Nova Scotian and Mi'kmaw communities, refugees and immigrants displaced by war, historians and other academics who study war and militarization, artists who respond to and reflect on their impact, and peace activists who vigorously protest against the militarization of the region. It is these stories, some told by new, previously unheard voices, that we want to highlight, while connecting them to the better-known accounts of military history.

The wide range of perspectives presented here underscores the far-reaching and perhaps unanticipated impacts of war on Nova Scotia, both historically and now. Geographic markers of war and militarization are common. The historic Fortress of Louisbourg and Fort Anne are two of the province's most popular tourist destinations, and the Halifax skyline continues to be dominated by Citadel Hill. The current military presence is equally apparent with Canadian Armed Forces bases dotted around the province, from CFB Cornwallis[1] in the Annapolis Valley to Victoria Park Armouries in Sydney, and with several bases in the Halifax region alone.

Nova Scotian society has also been marked by the impact of war for generations. Waves of immigrants and refugees have settled in Nova Scotia as a result of wars around the globe, and have contributed to this province's society and culture. The Acadian Deportation and Loyalist migrations were a result of wars fought elsewhere, which determined the settlement of Nova Scotia in the eighteenth and nineteenth centuries. One cannot understand Nova Scotia without recognizing the importance of the Black Loyalists who came to the province after the American War of Independence, the influx of war brides from Europe after the Second World War, the Lebanese migration during the Lebanese Civil War, the more recent arrival of refugees escaping civil war in Syria, or the new wave of refugees fleeing Ukraine due to the Russian invasion. Nova Scotia as a place and people intimately reflects the consequences of wars and armed conflicts globally.

Including these previously neglected voices and perspectives on war and peace in Nova Scotia not only recognizes their value, but also offers a more comprehensive understanding of the impact of war in our province. Moreover, bringing these voices together provides a way to bridge the divide between disparate communities. Military and civilian personnel, refugees, and peace activists may be impacted by armed conflict and militarization in quite different ways, yet they are intrinsically connected through their experiences. We hope that by highlighting these connections we can spur broader public debate on the issues of war and military activity, peacekeeping, and peace activism.

Our focus is on having members of a wide range of communities tell their stories because we believe storytelling matters. Storytelling is a way for us to comprehend our own experiences and identities. We also use stories to connect with and influence others. Stories of war and peace help us to make sense of history, and they expose the impacts and legacies of war in ways that may influence future policy decisions and shape potential alternatives to war.

Our initial goal was to explore what stories were being told in our communities. We wanted to know the stories of people who had been marginalized. In the process, we encountered challenges: How do we include the vital perspectives of communities reticent to tell their stories? How do we avoid reproducing dominant narratives, such as those depicting military spouses as self-sacrificing and those framing the refugee experience as one of salvation? How do we tell authentic stories that capture real-life challenges and victories? What is gained in telling these stories? What is lost? We ultimately navigated these challenges through our shared belief in the importance of storytelling—for individuals and communities, for history, and for future generations.

Those who share their stories in this collection do so for many reasons—to put words to what they have seen, to reflect on their experiences, to grapple with challenges, to tell, to teach, and to transform. They present their own perspectives and use their own voices—their own words and ways of speaking—whether it be in verse or song, rooted in realism or in abstraction and metaphor.[2] Some perspectives stand in opposition to one another; some challenge what is presented by mainstream media. It is important that they are all heard, as together they shape a more comprehensive and nuanced narrative about the impact and legacy of war and peace in Nova Scotia and, by extension, Canada. Some of these stories may make us uncomfortable—they will remind us of Canada's, and Nova Scotia's, history of racism and discrimination. They will remind us of the atrocities of war. Discomfort, however, can be productive. It can spark important conversations and lead to action. All we ask is for you to listen to what our contributors have to say.

The collection is loosely divided into three parts: stories of the present—from veterans, military family members, and refugees living in the province; stories of the past—military histories and accounts of experiences in the two world wars; and stories of resistance and reflections on war and military practices from activists and artists. These divisions, though, belie the connections between them: how the resilience of those who experienced the Halifax Explosion, say, echoes the resilience of a refugee from Syria; how the sacrifice and unacknowledged labour of family members of military personnel is little changed from a century ago; how members of certain communities have been prevented from being part of the Canadian military, whether it was African Nova Scotians a century ago or those of the 2SLGBTQIA+ community as recently as thirty years ago.

We begin with stories of present-day military veterans—what might be considered part of the dominant military narrative. Certainly, the primary understanding of the term veteran may be of a war or combat veteran; however, chapter one demonstrates the diversity of veteran experience, from the rewards and challenges of military service to the difficulties of reintegrating into civilian society, and the impact of the Canadian government's LGBT Purge that started in the 1950s and lasted well into the 1990s.

Chapter two also broadens our understanding of military personnel by considering the impact of war and military activity on their families. Families of military members are essential to the armed forces' ability to operate, yet their stories are often ignored because of the concept of family as private and secondary to the member's service. This chapter, which includes contributions by a researcher and a military spouse, underscores the need for us to expand our definition of family and to recognize the labour of military spouses.

Continuing the exploration of how people in Nova Scotia today are affected by war and peace, chapter three tells the stories of four individuals who were forced to migrate to the province because of violence, political persecution, or war. Their stories reflect the unprecedented global humanitarian crises that forcibly displace twenty-five people every minute—half of them children. These stories counter the anti-refugee narrative that focuses on security and economic concerns and encourages fear of the "dangerous other." They demonstrate the resilience of people who make sacrifices to protect their families and communities and who dream of a world where everyone's human rights are respected.

With chapter four, we turn our attention from present-day experiences to historic accounts of the impact of war and peace on diverse communities and how this history continues to affect Nova Scotia today. The chapter examines African Nova Scotians' involvement in war with a particular focus on the First World War, when the community was actively demanding the right to defend

Canada through military service. In response, the No. 2 Construction Battalion, known as the Black Battalion, was formed in Pictou, NS. This historic event is then connected to the community's ongoing participation in building and defending Canada and how the makeup of the Canadian military in the twentieth and twenty-first centuries illustrates the diaspora of people of African descent throughout the Americas.

In chapter five, we showcase diverse military histories, from the more well-known accounts to those of the Mi'kmaw and Acadian communities, focusing on the impact of the First and Second World Wars. Contributors emphasize the personal cost and human sacrifice that come with war, as well as the challenge of uncovering previously unheard military histories and the importance of documenting them for future generations.

Chapter six brings together voices from the Mi'kmaw and African Nova Scotian communities and their experiences of the 1917 Halifax Explosion, experiences that have been ignored until recently. Focusing on the events of the centenary of the 1917 Halifax Explosion, these voices are set alongside those of researchers, artists, and designers who examine how certain communities were razed and erased by the explosion and its aftermath, how our understanding of events changes with each new discovery, and how we can commemorate the event in a way that acknowledges all the communities affected.

From a discussion of how war has shaped Nova Scotia's land and people for much of the province's history, we move, in chapter seven, to hear the voices of peace activists who have protested against war and militarization. The province has a rich history of peace activism that is often overshadowed by its dominant military narrative. That history is outlined here—from the peace activism of the First World War to the Cold War Pugwash movement and the more recent efforts of the Halifax Peace Coalition. As in the other chapters, there is a diversity of perspectives, ranging from that of a military veteran opposed to nuclear arms to those of a US war resister, a member of the women's peace movement, and a spoken word artist who participates in ongoing peace demonstrations in Halifax today.

Chapter eight also considers responses to war and military conflict by examining how war has shaped the art that surrounds us. The chapter focuses on art in public spaces in Nova Scotia—namely commemorative statues and monuments and their function as war memorials. Contributors explore how monuments often tell only one version of a military conflict—that of the victor—and how counter-monuments, which draw attention to themselves and encourage people to explore the space they occupy, may provide room for additional points of view. This chapter, like that on the Halifax Explosion, reminds us of how our landscape is irrevocably marked by war.

We close the collection with a consideration of the relationship between weaving and storytelling, drawing on Mi'kmaw insights about the two activities. Such insights stress the importance of relational knowledge and community-building through storytelling, while recognizing the challenges of bringing stories—and people—together.

It is our hope that these wide-ranging stories of war and peace will encourage you to recognize the tremendous impact war and militarization have had, and continue to have, on Nova Scotia. It is our belief that hearing about the experiences of others—particularly when told in their own voices—creates greater understanding and will help to bridge the gaps that often exist between diverse communities. Our goal is for this collection to spark a deeper conversation between Nova Scotians of all backgrounds about the impacts of war and peace, particularly because it is only by knowing and reflecting on the past and present that we can prepare for the future.

NOTES

1 Canadian Forces Bases will be abbreviated to CFB throughout this book as that is how they are usually presented to the public.

2 While great care has been taken to preserve contributors' own words and ways of speaking whenever possible, some of the contributions based on transcribed interviews have been lightly edited to clarify the speakers' intended meaning.

Chapter 1

Military Veterans

Introduction

Maya Eichler

Colloquially, Canadians associate the term *veteran* with an older generation. However, a new generation of veterans of the post–Cold War period has emerged as the population of Second World War and Korean War veterans declines. Since the 1990s, the Canadian Armed Forces have deployed to countless conflict zones, including the former Yugoslavia, Afghanistan, and Mali. As a result, veteran issues have re-emerged as a major concern, with the government, media, and civil society paying increased attention to modern-day veterans and their transition from military to civilian life. The question of who gets to claim the title of *veteran* remains a contentious one, and is often linked to length and type of service. Often, women veterans are less likely to be recognized as veterans or to feel like they can whole-heartedly embrace a veteran identity. Veteran status is often conflated with combat or deployment experience. In this chapter, we use the term *veteran* in an inclusive way to refer to people who have served in the military regardless of their service history.

Countless media stories have highlighted veteran struggles with mental health, homelessness, and insufficient services. These stories hit home in Nova Scotia, particularly in view of the 2018 tragedy in Upper Big Tracadie in which an Afghanistan veteran took the lives of his daughter, wife, mother, and himself. While this is an especially tragic case, it highlights the challenges experienced by veterans and their families not only during but after military service. It is also in Nova Scotia that many grassroots efforts *by* veterans *for* veterans have emerged. For example, VETS Canada, now a national organization aimed at addressing veteran homelessness, began its work and continues to be headquartered here in Dartmouth. Another example, one featured in this chapter, is the Veteran Farm Project located outside Windsor, NS. It aims to improve the health and well-being of veterans by offering them an opportunity to be in nature and grow food. At the same time, it provides veterans experiencing food insecurity with fresh produce.

Today's veterans face particular challenges. They are leaving the military at a younger age and are more likely than past veterans to be released for medical reasons. That means a significant number of veterans deal with the challenges of transitioning from military to civilian life while also having to manage an injury or illness. About one in four veterans is released from the military for medical reasons (Thompson and Lockhart 2015). Roughly one-third report a difficult adjustment to civilian life (Van Til *et al.* 2017).

In public discourse, veterans are framed in contradictory ways as both heroes and victims, but there is often not much understanding of their lived experience. For many veterans, the term *transition* does not adequately capture the experience of post-service life, as the military identity is never completely shed. The lack of a clear-cut modern-day veteran identity to step into, coupled with the gap between military and civilian spheres, presents a challenge for veterans trying to transition to civilian life. Veterans highlight the strange cross-cultural encounters that occur between ex-military members and civilians. Military and civilian worlds use different expressions and have different expectations. Military culture itself is interpreted as both a benefit and a hindrance. As a benefit, skills acquired in the military context, such as a strong work ethic and organizational habits, help with the ensuing transition to civilian life. Finding civilian jobs in military-related areas and institutions provides an avenue for some veterans to transition while staying connected to their military identity.

Veterans speak of how entering the military entails an intense period of socialization that transforms them into military members, yet there is no equivalent preparation for their return to civilian life. For many, the military experience happens early in their adult life, shaping them profoundly as individuals. It is not an identity that can be easily shed when releasing or retiring from service. John Whelan, who tells his story in this chapter, is a veteran and psychologist who has spent his career working with military members and veterans. In his reflection "Vagabonds Among You," Whelan shares how he came into military service, and how his time in the military has forever altered his sense of belonging and his relationship to home. Central to Whelan's narrative are the ideas of transiency and alienation—how veterans can feel a sense of disconnect from civilian society due to lack of supports and understanding. In "Finding a New Purpose," Ken Hoffer, a thirty-year veteran of the Royal Canadian Navy, revisits defining moments in his service life. Hoffer offers a portrait of a military career marked by moments of trauma and hopelessness as well as deep personal fulfillment. Exploring what it means to find one's purpose, in and out of military service, this narrative illustrates the multifaceted ways in which military members imagine service and military identity.

As we pay attention to this new generation of veterans, it is important to recognize that there are many veteran experiences. Unfortunately, existing support structures often do not address the specific needs of veterans who do not fit the norm of the white, heterosexual, cisgender male veteran. In a 2019 piece in the *Globe and Mail* titled "We Are the Invisible: The Problem with How We Understand Our Veterans," veteran Kelly S. Thompson challenges readers to embrace the diversity of veteran experiences that include those of racialized veterans, women veterans, and immigrant veterans. We share this sentiment and take the opportunity to highlight the often-marginalized experiences of women veterans.

In this chapter, Jessica Miller shares her story "Creating the Veteran Farm Project." Having spent more than twenty years in the military, she had to leave unexpectedly as a result of multiple physical injuries. As a woman veteran and survivor of military sexual trauma, it was important to her to create a space that is welcoming to veterans like herself. The Veteran Farm Project offers primarily women veterans a space to connect with nature and support veterans facing food insecurities while finding a path toward their own healing and transition to civilian life.

This chapter also highlights the experiences of lesbian and gay veterans, specifically in the context of the Cold War Purge. The Purge was a campaign of discrimination and persecution conducted by the federal government against public servants suspected of being homosexual. Beginning in the 1950s, it lasted into the early 1990s (Kinsman and Gentile 2010) and had a particular impact on military members serving in Nova Scotia. This chapter deliberately uses a variety of terms and acronyms, such as LGBT Purge, LGBTQ2 apology, LGBTQ+, and gays and lesbians, to reflect particular historic and personal contexts and changes in official usage of language in relation to events and experiences involving the 2SLGBTQIA+ community.

"Feminist Military Veteran and LGBT Purge Survivor" by Darl Wood, Carmen Poulin, and Lynne Gouliquer, is a piece co-written by a Purge survivor, a civilian academic, and a veteran academic. It tells the story of Wood, whose military career was cut short as a result of government-sanctioned, systemic discrimination. She was investigated, mistreated, and dishonourably discharged because of her sexual orientation. That trauma and her feminist convictions have underpinned the important work she has engaged in ever since, including in the women's peace movement. Through her social activism, teaching, and political involvement, Wood has contributed significantly to Nova Scotia's rich and vibrant history.

"Being Gay and Ex-Military in Nova Scotia" presents a conversation between Frank Letourneau, a navy veteran forced to resign in 1970 when confronted with evidence of his homosexuality, and Maya Eichler. Although many thousands of gay and lesbian military members and public servants were impacted by the Canadian government's explicitly homophobic policy, the LGBT Purge remains a relatively unknown aspect of Canadian history among the general public. In this interview, Letourneau offers valuable insight into a story not often told, sharing his experience of serving in the navy as a gay man, his forced resignation, and his understanding of events more than fifty years later.

Today's veterans have diverse backgrounds and experiences of military service, though—like the rest of us—they share life's struggles of confronting social injustices and finding purpose. Members of this generation of veterans are seeking new ways of organizing and building community in order to have their voices heard and to address gaps in service delivery. They are less likely to be involved with traditional organizations such as the Royal Canadian Legion and, instead, are heavily reliant on social media. This chapter, we hope, can help narrow the military–civilian divide and increase our collective understanding of the diverse experiences of veterans as they transition to civilian life.

Vagabonds Among You

John Whelan

As a former member of the military and a psychologist in Nova Scotia, I am like many military people and veterans who live here. For the most part, we are transients and transplants to the province. I grew up in Newfoundland and arrived in 1977 as a twenty-year-old recruit in the Royal Canadian Navy. I came from a large Irish Catholic family with a military history beginning in the First World War and lasting up to the present. I heard stories from my uncle about the British Royal Navy during the Second World War and about my birthplace, Bell Island, being attacked by German U-boats during that war. These stories and the movie scenes of Canadian corvettes and their iconic blaring action alarms are part of my earliest memories.

As a teenager, however, the images and the sounds of the US–Vietnam War and the dead and mutilated civilians and soldiers had a profound effect on me. The images of young men not much older than me jumping from helicopters into lush vegetation in brilliant sunshine amid explosions and gunfire are seared in my memory. I was struck and deeply saddened by the incongruity and brutality of it all—there was no glory that I could see. I was an A student, involved in sports; I hunted, and I was street-smart, having learned to fight to protect myself as a kid. But I also lived in a poor province with few opportunities and decided to leave home to join the military. Recruit training at CFB Cornwallis followed by a posting to Halifax opened up a world centred around military life.

I learned about the history of Halifax as a navy town, the vast convoys in Bedford Basin during the Second World War, the military history of Aldershot and Debert, and the devastation caused by the Halifax Explosion. I trained at the leftover facilities at Osborne Head, Newport Corner, York Redoubt, and Mill Cove and visited the forts and forgotten Second World War gun placements at McNabs Island, Citadel Hill, and Point Pleasant. And like my home province of Newfoundland—which commemorates the slaughter of its young men at Beaumont-Hamel on July 1 every year—Nova Scotians also remembered the many people they had lost to various wars.

Beyond these military roots, however, people on the streets of Halifax, like today, had very few direct connections to or little awareness of the military. We learned to stick together and to be wary of civilians in our home port of Halifax, just like we did in foreign ports. One of my close friends was badly beaten and hospitalized, and another friend was stabbed outside the main gate of CFB Halifax. We were told about how the navy had let the sailors loose on the streets of Halifax in the 1960s to exact justice for ongoing beatings and robberies. Walking inside the navy dockyard in Halifax or onboard the ship in foreign ports meant safety from the civilian world. We were a culture unto ourselves. I still have mixed thoughts about Halifax and about civilians. The world of business and ordinary life means that the military is rarely noticed by the general public.

I made various attempts to return home, but I realized that there was no going back to who I was before the military. After the military, I focused on re-inventing myself in academia and learning to mimic other professionals. I have been practicing in the province as a psychologist since the early 1990s, working with military members and veterans. I know of no other psychologists in Nova Scotia with military service, which has left me as an outsider.

When it comes to service in war zones, nations have always grappled with the problem of re-integrating men and women infected by the horrors of war. While the discipline of psychology owes its success to the study of soldiers who served in the Second World War, the things we were taught do not reflect the experiences of modern-day soldiers and veterans. During the height of the war in Afghanistan, I assessed and treated hundreds of men and women devastated by the things they had seen and done in Canada's name. Many of them felt betrayed by the military and forgotten by civilian society. There was so much anger and despair to manage that it simply wore me down mentally and emotionally. To my surprise, my military service offered few protections—in fact, it made me acutely aware of the anger and emptiness in those I saw and the indifference of our federal bureaucracies.

Canadians, including our politicians and the military leadership, grew tired of Afghanistan and wanted to move on. Veterans seemed to be screaming in anger and despair over what they had lost of themselves—but nobody was listening to them. We were taught that war trauma was a sign of compromised brains, but this theory missed the fact that veterans had no place to tell their stories—no place to call home. We psychologists and other helpers were doing our best to help them to forget war, but we had no ideas about how to reconnect with community—any community. Veterans did what they knew best: they reformed their subcultures across Canada to reconnect with each other. But many of them still have not come home—they are outsiders among their military friends, among older veterans, and within their families and neighbourhoods. Unfortunately, I do not believe that Canadians know how to make room for their returning sons and daughters.

It is not that people are mean-spirited, but these soldiers and veterans are cast aside and forgotten as we move on collectively. Instead, citizens gather under monuments and give passing acknowledgments to the military as a national icon. Few people, including professionals working with the veteran community, take the time to understand life inside the military organization—what is required to take on its values and mission and what is required to relinquish them when we leave.

I have learned important lessons from my military friends and veterans over the years. It is easy to be patriotic and wave flags when there is nothing on the line. It is an entirely different matter to give one's soul to that cause when it costs people everything they have. And when people realize the costs of their own inhumanity, they become strangers unto themselves and strangers to everyone else. Many of them, including myself, must accept that we are transients in the communities we end up living in.

When people ask me where I am from these days, the true answer is that I really don't know—maybe I haven't known since leaving home as a young man. I have lived in Nova Scotia for over forty years, raised a family here, and have people I call my friends. I move comfortably in professional and community circles, but I also can leave them easily and just move on—a vagabond.

Finding a New Purpose

Ken Hoffer

I could feel the perspiration trickle down my back as I stood with my fellow sailors—staring at the black greasy spot on the ground where the remains of over thirty men, women, and children had been unceremoniously piled in a heap and set ablaze. The locals had since enshrined their fallen, encircling the cremation site with a ring of white stones and orange flowers. The intense tropical heat and humidity amplified the smell of burned flesh and blood that soaked the ground. This extermination site was the work of Indonesian Defence Forces and civilian militias, which also included teens who were forced into service. On September 4, 1999, the Indonesian militias set into action a carefully staged plan to rape, pillage, and burn the Christian communities in the newly declared nation-state of East Timor. We arrived in late October 1999. Our ship, HMCS *Protecteur*, was anchored in turquoise seas just half a mile offshore, near the village of Suai. We were standing in a burned-out Catholic school compound where one of the most horrific atrocities had occurred during that nightmarish week in September.

My attention was drawn back to the sickening sight of teeth and cremated skull fragments protruding from the tarry mess. Amplifying the horror, we could see the personal effects belonging to those whose lives had been snuffed out. Stuck in the black ooze: a partially melted pink hair comb, a scorched pair of men's wire-rim glass frames, a burned shoe, a charred watch face, a child's blue flip-flop, and a small charred, headless doll. One of the sailors turned to me and spoke, "Sir, why are we here? Why do we have to see this?"

My mind raced back to mid-September 1999 when we were first informed that we had only ten days to prepare the ship and crew to sail for a small island called East Timor. None of us had any idea where the island was located in the South Pacific, nor did we have any sense of the history, language, culture, or the current geopolitical situation that necessitated the mobilization of a Canadian task force to deploy on a peace-support operation to the country. We only knew we were heading into a potentially hot war zone. While we scrambled to gain information and intelligence on our mission, our can-do exuberance to make haste with our pre-deployment training and preparations was dampened by the inevitability of going home to inform our families.

We are not trained to deal with the profound psychological effects of deployment—of entering a war zone and leaving behind our families. When I told my wife and kids that I was leaving for a war zone, you could see the tears begin to well. These are foreboding moments for all involved, marked by the knowledge that going off to war brings increased risk. Military families suffer profound stress knowing that they could lose a loved one during hostilities. That fear smoulders silently in every soldier, sailor, and aviator. I was an executive officer (second-in-command), so the ship's crew was also my family. I knew that the anxiety I shared with my own family over our dinner table that evening was also present in every crew member's household and in the homes of every other military member across Canada who had received their orders to deploy that day. We were going into harm's way, and I wasn't confident that I, or any of my crew, was psychologically prepared for what we were about to encounter.

My attention focused back on the killing ground. As I gazed across the compound, I could see the blood-soaked handprints raking down the cinder-block walls where the priests and villagers ran and pleaded for their lives to be spared. Bullet holes pierced the walls of a burned-out chapel and the raw concrete walls of a cathedral under construction. Innocent victims were slaughtered here. One could imagine the echoes of gunfire and screams that occurred on this holy ground.

I looked into the distressed faces of my sailors. I spoke in a steady and firm tone, "Gentlemen, we are here to help this nation and to help this community overcome the injustices brutally inflicted upon them. We can help them rebuild and get back to some level of normality. This is who we are as Canadians. We are here to help...let's get on with it!"

Over the next three months, our task force helped to sustain the International Force in East Timor. Our ship also worked with UN representatives and NGOs to help rebuild a police station in Dili, to support Doctors Without Borders with helicopter airlifts to remote villages, and to rebuild schoolrooms, a chapel, and a market in the village of Suai. Our tradespersons helped to re-establish the water supply and electrical generators to power key infrastructure facilities. Our ship also delivered diesel fuel to East Timor. We could see that we were pumping life back into society. Electrical power was gradually restored. The flickering cooking fires that dotted the hills when we first arrived had faded away in the glow of electric lights.

The most profound effect of our humanitarian support was reflected in the eyes of the men, women, and children in Suai. The community came alive, school classes resumed, the market was bustling, and the power of faith within the community helped to energize and motivate the populace to rise from the ashes. We focused on supporting the community, liaising with village elders, priests, teachers, families, and NGOs to cater to their immediate needs.

Unfortunately, the Canadian mission in East Timor was cut short. We returned to our home base in Esquimalt, BC, with mixed feelings that our mission was not complete. Canadian political decisions to contribute military resources to deployed operations are not necessarily based on a sound foreign policy to promote human security or provide humanitarian support. The electorate in Canada is generally supportive of these missions from an ethical and moral point of view. Unfortunately, efforts to deploy high-readiness forces and sustain operations to their end state are often severely underfunded. This was the situation in East Timor. Our Canadian task force was an ad-hoc collection of resources, but it was able to provide a significant contribution to the International Force in East Timor through its can-do initiative.

Eighteen months later, I found myself standing on a stage in an auditorium at CFB Kingston, ON. I was now the chief of staff for the Joint Operations Group. As I was speaking about our program for pre-deployment training, our chaplain entered and announced that a plane had flown into the World Trade Center in New York City. I had just mentioned to the 156 personnel who were present that we could be asked to deploy with less than forty-eight hours' notice. Thirty-six hours later, I found myself on a flight to the Central Command headquarters in Tampa, Florida, to commence the planning for Canada's commitment to the US-led war on terror in Afghanistan. Once again, my family and other families across Canada were feeling the trepidation and vulnerability at the possibility of losing a loved one in hostile action in a foreign land.

This time was different. Canadians would die and suffer serious physical and mental health injuries in combat. I wondered how many casualties Canadians would accept before they petitioned their members of parliament to withdraw. How much would the government invest in new equipment and in the training and preparation of personnel to ensure the Canadian military was fully capable of sustained operations? Although significant gains were made there in creating schools and medical services and establishing protective security, Canada withdrew from a campaign where no end state was achieved. The corruption, tribal feuds, and terrorist activities are still present, twenty-one years after Canada's initial involvement following the 9/11 attacks.

I often hear from veterans who deployed to Afghanistan that they feel morally cheated. There is a sense that the overall mission was unsuccessful, that we abandoned the vulnerable population at a critical turning point. This moral dejection coupled with the severe trauma that some soldiers experienced in fierce combat situations has a profound effect on the mental health of an individual, often resulting in PTSD, which can manifest immediately or years after the fact. Veterans released from the Canadian Armed Forces can also feel a lost sense of purpose. Hanging up the uniform after a successful career in the military can be an overwhelming experience unless the individual has created a new and rewarding career path. Some veterans move on to corporate management positions; others redefine their military skill sets to appeal to civilian employers; still others choose to venture into new entrepreneurial activities or simply to retire and enjoy creative or recreational activities with family and friends. For those individuals who have no life plan, and/or suffer from PTSD, it can be difficult to make the transition back to civilian life. They feel there is no purpose for them when, in fact, there is much value in repurposing their professional skills in ways that can contribute to their community.

The experience of many operational deployments and my strategic appreciation of ongoing global security issues left me with doubts as to whether my lengthy time away from family was worth the personal sacrifice. I would be the first to admit that I chose my career path and, therefore, accept the consequences of that decision. In 2016, I was fortunate to find a new purpose. I applied for and was accepted into the first cohort of Veteran Trainers to Eradicate the Use of Child Soldiers (VTECS). The program was offered through the Roméo Dallaire Child Soldier Initiative, which is based at Dalhousie University, Halifax. The VTECS program offers former members of the Canadian Armed Forces an opportunity to repurpose their knowledge and skills to help prevent the recruitment and use of child soldiers. As veterans, we continue to uphold our entrusted obligations to protect and promote Canadian ideals that will deter belligerents from dehumanizing civilians, especially children, in all theatres of operation. As VTECS members, we uphold these values and realize that we have become part of a larger vision to interrupt the cycle of hate and violence.

I rely on my wealth of personal and military experience and expertise, in conjunction with the education and skills I developed through the VTECS program, to conduct pre-deployment training for military and police battalions. I have been privileged to be deployed to Sierra Leone, Kenya, Uganda, and Rwanda to work with their security forces. In my mind, I could not simply retire to my comfy recliner and hide from the realities of contemporary conflict. I still feel the need to be part of the security sector solution to make the world a better place. The VTECS program gave me the opportunity to discover a new purpose in my life.

Creating the Veteran Farm Project

Jessica Miller

I'm from Ontario. I grew up in a town called Aurora. In 1997, there was a program through my high school where you could earn four high-school credits for completing basic military training, sort of like a co-op placement. I had a boyfriend at the time who was doing it, and I thought, "That sounds cool. I want to do that, too." And he said, "No way." I was stubborn and didn't like someone telling me there was something I couldn't do, so I said, "Yes, I'm doing it." That's how it started. I did basic training while I was in high school.

Originally, I joined as an armoured crewman. I didn't understand the different trades that were available, so I just did what everyone else was doing. I had no idea what I was joining. My mum was a nurse, and I had thought about becoming a paramedic. As it happened, I was presented an opportunity to become a medical assistant, was whisked off for training at CFB Borden, and was on course to become a medic.

I was in my last semester of high school when the big ice storm hit Eastern Ontario in 1998. I was called up to head out there to help those affected by the storm. It was my first experience helping others in a traumatic situation, and I thrived in that environment. I just fell in love with what I was doing and kept going along with it from there. I was a reservist for more than eleven years, and then I joined the Regular Force and stayed for another eleven years.

There were ups and downs. I enjoyed a lot of aspects of military service. There were certainly times I didn't enjoy, and some I wish I could forget. I went to Afghanistan as a reservist on the very first tour, Roto 0, Operation Athena. It was a very scary and difficult mission. After my return from Afghanistan, I joined the Regular Force, was posted to Halifax, and was given the opportunity to sail. I've had mixed feelings about my career, for sure. Being a woman in the military was difficult. As a medic I worked with many female service members. It is a trade with a lot of females. In that sense, it was good. There were other women to be with, but it was a very male-dominated environment.

Military life is complicated because, even when you're in a leadership position—I was a sergeant when I was released—and you're supposed to be in charge, there's always that man who will question you. It's a difficult one to wrap your head around. When I was practicing as a medic and treating patients, gender didn't play a role. But as soon as I stepped outside of that, it absolutely hung over everything else I had to do in the forces. There was always a balance of being not too feminine but also not too masculine. You had to laugh at the guys' jokes, but not be too crude at the same time. You had to put up with it or you were not one of them. There's always that balance, and you're always trying to find how you can fit in with whatever men you're around at the time.

In 2018, I was medically released from the military. I had a couple of bad accidents while I was on ship. I broke my back and had two spinal fusions, and then I broke my hip. I didn't have much of a choice. I physically couldn't do the work anymore. If I hadn't been medically released, I would still be in the military. My last posting was here in Nova Scotia. I had spent the last ten years of my military career here and I wanted to stay after my release.

I think it doesn't matter how long you have served: anyone who has served probably has that innate feeling of needing to help, to give back, to support those who are less fortunate or injured or ill. I know for me, that's what my job was as a medic in the military. I couldn't just let that go. And that's how the Veteran Farm Project started. I was still in the military when I purchased this property only thirty minutes outside of Halifax. I didn't know what it was going to be, but something in me said, *I have to buy this property. Now what?* It's been a lot of work. My spouse and I were plugging away at that for the first year. I was growing some vegetables, and a friend of mine, whose husband was involved in a lot of veteran advocacy, asked if we had any extra for some seniors who were experiencing food insecurity. So, I packaged some up and I sent them with her. They were grateful, and it felt good to be able to provide.

Unfortunately, we do have a big food insecurity problem within the veteran community. Over the winter of 2018, I got this idea and I put it together as a proposal to provide food boxes through the Royal Canadian Legion (Nova Scotia Command). Our first year was 2019, and we were successful beyond what I thought we could do. We were able to support ten families—over sixty people—with food weekly for three months.

What we do is we put together a box with the produce we grow, and then we add pantry staples, like dried pasta, and put in a recipe so people can make a full meal and learn about a new vegetable. The boxes are delivered weekly to the Legion and then picked up by the families. We received an email from one of the recipients who said he was on the verge of dying by suicide until he received one of our care packages, and he realized there were people out there who care. We received a bunch of feedback like that. It made me feel like there's a niche that needed to be filled.

But the Veteran Farm Project is also a way to support women and women veterans specifically. In my service, I experienced sexual trauma, both from somebody I worked with and from my chain of command, which left me uncomfortable working around men and being around men who I don't know. In order to help myself not fall into the trap of depression—a lot of veterans do—I felt I needed to do something. First off, there was nothing out there for me. So, I thought, well, if there's nothing for me, then there must be other women who don't have anything. That just kind of got me thinking:

Why don't we do something for women? So, the idea is therapeutic horticulture—not horticultural therapy, because I'm not a therapist—taking the principles that you learn, either through therapy or through personal experience, and translating those into real-life improvements. You find grounding through having your hands in the dirt and connecting, watching plants grow, seeing the changes as the season goes, and meeting other women.

All of a sudden, there was me and another woman veteran, and then next thing you know, we had twelve of us, and I was like, "Wow. I didn't realize there were so many." Our drop-in day is Wednesday, so we have women drop by then. We basically heal and go through the journey of becoming whoever or whatever we're going to be post-service through the farm, and then the by-product of that is that we grow all these vegetables. We don't share experiences or talk about our traumas much because that's what therapy is for. It's more about being able to come together. We provide a safe space for women whose needs aren't being met in Nova Scotia, or across Canada. And that was one of the priorities—creating a safe place for women to come together and just be together.

There is a huge gap when it comes to transitioning out of the forces. They just say, "Here's your veteran ID card, and thank you for your service." There is no transition. There's Veterans Affairs, but you are still left to transition on your own, which is crazy. When you join at eighteen and leave at forty, you don't know what you are supposed to be doing or who you are supposed to be, or how any of this stuff works. Using the term *veteran* for our project wasn't so much for myself because I would definitely say, on a normal day, I don't refer to myself as a veteran. I don't wear anything that would indicate that I was in the forces. Naming the project "The Veteran Farm Project" was hard because it was hard for me to actually say that I am a veteran. I think I did it more for everyone else because a lot of the women—they don't feel like veterans.

This is something I take a lot of pride in—recognizing that there's a gap for women veterans and that we are addressing it. We need to look after our women veterans better than we do, because we're not doing a good job. Even with the large population of veterans we have in Nova Scotia, there is still that missing piece for women. If we can find a way to engage more women veterans and make them feel safe and that they belong, it will improve their mental health. And then, in turn, through our farm, they get healthy physically with good nutrition and the experiences on the farm. The power of being in nature and doing something for someone else—it's medicinal in a way that you can't describe.

Feminist Military Veteran and LGBT Purge Survivor

Darl Wood, with Carmen Poulin and Lynne Gouliquer

PROLOGUE

In 1978, Darl Wood was released from the military for homosexuality. She fought to tell the world of this injustice for years. Wood's efforts make her one of the pioneers in the fight for the rights of marginalized groups in Canada. The LGBT Purge class action settlement and the Canadian Government's apology to the LGBTQ2 community in December 2017 came about because of people like Wood. Although she is proud of this accomplishment, her contributions to the feminist peace movement through her involvement in the Nova Scotia Voice of Women for Peace and the Canadian Voice of Women for Peace also bring her much satisfaction. Here is her story in her own words.

"ONE CAN NEVER REALLY GET AWAY FROM NOVA SCOTIA"

I was born in Truro on January 4, 1951. I loved my family very much, but growing up, I needed to distance myself from them. I also had the sense that nobody really left Nova Scotia. I felt trapped. So, when I turned eighteen, with pennies in my pockets, I took off to go out west. I headed out with my best buddy, who was also my cousin. We were off on an adventure. Unfortunately, I caught pneumonia and had to return to Truro where my mother nursed me back to health. Not long after, we got the news that my cousin had killed himself. His suicide left me devastated and shocked.

INFLUENTIAL INSTITUTIONS—THE MILITARY AND RELIGION

Following my cousin's suicide, I desperately needed structure and predictability. I attended business college but I did not want to be a secretary. What I had really wanted to go into was computer sciences.

Back then, however, women did not become programmers. I finished business college, and then I enrolled in the military. It provided structure and guidance. Although it was the military, it could just as easily have been religion. My father had served in the Second World War, and yet I don't know much about his experience. One of my brothers joined the military before going into the ministry; one of my two younger sisters joined a few months after I did, and the other one became a minister. In fact, she is close to completing her PhD in religious studies. One of my older sisters married a minister and the other one became a missionary. Our religious background was Baptist evangelical, and in the name of religious mores and proscription, we had many rules to follow, but the military also came with its own set of rules and regulations.

When it came to religion, ironically, my mother helped me move beyond the strict constraints of patriarchally organized religions. One day, I was driving her to an appointment, and she said to me, "Now I suppose you're going to tell me that God is a woman?" I don't think she realized that her question put me on the road to women's spirituality and to resolving my sexual and religious orientations. How I would resolve my religious beliefs and sexual orientation once I was in the military, however, was more complicated.

MY MILITARY EXPERIENCE

In the 1970s, there was a real push to have women in the military. I was too short, too skinny, and yet I was accepted to join the air force. I remember the long ride from Truro to Halifax to take the tests and then off we went to Cornwallis. One minute I was meeting people who were different from me, and the next minute, we were all dressed the same with the same uniforms and the same haircuts. It was instant camaraderie. They had taken every personal item that made us unique—everything we knew up until that point.

People forget about one part of the military: the part that turns everyone into a killing machine. They had to kill the woman in each one of us. It was pretty awful. I guess those are the things you just set aside. You bury them somehow, but for me, they remained a source of conflict. I loved the women I met in the military, but I hated militarism.

THE MILITARY AND HOMOSEXUALITY

People love the military because they get the feeling of belonging and camaraderie. You can't put a group of people together, however, and not expect intimate relationships to develop. Even between heterosexual women, they have that love, that camaraderie. I did not think of it as sexual, at least not until I met my first woman lover. You have that sense of doing something exciting, working toward a common goal. Yet, ambivalent feelings would haunt me because some people were mistreated. Individuals were taken away to a special room and given a lecture. Although we weren't privy to its content, we all knew it was about homosexuality.

Until I started a relationship with a woman, I did not feel like it was affecting me. Then one day, a woman who was being released for homosexuality came out to me. It was the first time someone had spoken to me openly about their sexual orientation. Although I was having these feelings for women, I found myself speaking to her about religion and God. I wish I could take back this homophobic moment.

I got through boot camp and went on to CFB Borden for training as an administrative clerk. I was then transferred to Windsor Park, CFB Halifax. In my military job, reports of people being investigated and discharged were coming across my desk. I started to recognize the names. So, I knew what was happening. I knew of the consequences. Once someone was investigated, no one would associate with that person. But, if I knew the person being released, I would go and sit with them, even though I was afraid. We were all living in fear, but I refused to isolate people.

MEETING MY FIRST WOMAN LOVER

It was 1977 when I met Maggie in Stadacona, CFB Halifax. She was a sergeant in the naval reserves, popular and funny. Everyone in the unit was excited about her coming for the summer. I had heard stories about her. One night after work, I was winding down in the barracks' lounge area, and Maggie walked in. She came up to me and said, "So, you're Darl Wood!" I just answered, "Yeah. Who the hell are you?" And that was Maggie. From that moment on, we were together 24-7. Although the attraction was immediate, I didn't exactly know what it was…but she did, and she was right. Eventually, she moved in with me. It was summer; I was involved in sports, and Maggie would join us after the games at the junior rank mess, that is, the bar. We were all living in fear, but we were young and in love. Unfortunately, I eventually got transferred to the military police unit.

GETTING KICKED OUT

Not long after the transfer, my major called me into the office out of the blue. I have no idea who talked but he asked me if I was involved with someone, if I was a "homosexual." Maggie and I had previously discussed this and had decided that we were not ashamed of who we were and that we would just come out if investigated. So, I just answered, "Yes." I was so naive. I was ordered over to the Special Investigation Unit across the road. I knew the guys. They took me to a shack and interrogated me. It was a little room with a straight-back cold metal chair, a table, and a dangling light. It was an out-of-body experience. I remember the panic surging through me. They wanted explicit details of a sexual nature: who, what, when, where, how. All I would repeat was that we were involved. But they kept asking the same questions over and over and over again. I think I got some water at one point. It took me years before I recognized that what they did was an assault, a sexual assault. The details of that day are still hazy. It lasted all day. I never got to clear out my office. My last act of military service was to type out my own discharge papers, and they officially read, "unadvantageously employable."

"MY LIFE JUST GOT INTERESTING"

One day, I saw a book in the garbage and noticed the title: *Flying* (by Kate Millett). I picked it up. It blew me away. The book answered my questions about what the military was doing. It made such an impact on my life and shifted me from depression to finding answers, and it steered me toward feminism.

At that time, anybody could secure government jobs, but I was told not to bother applying. This was also around the time of the CFB Shelburne bust when so many military women were discharged for homosexuality. I started writing about them in the press, which is when I knew my phone was being tapped; I could hear the distinctive clicks. Although I was no longer in the military, the military did not leave me alone. Always when I thought I had set it to rest, something would come up: somebody would want an interview or a presentation. Each time I'm on Parliament Hill, on national television, doing panels or writing articles, it evokes a form of retraumatization.

Feminists such as Linda Christiansen-Ruffman and Muriel Duckworth played an important part in my life. I would be nowhere without these amazing women. They are the reason I returned to university. Under Christiansen-Ruffman's guidance, I wrote my master's thesis on how lesbians took part in core feminist groups and what they did and did not do in order to fit in. I then trained and worked as a psychotherapist and, after working on a PhD in Women's Studies at York University, I taught as a university professor. Becoming a feminist helped me make sense of it all. My involvement in the feminist peace movement allowed me to explore feminist spirituality, which was such a different experience from religiosity. I also became involved in the Voice of Women for Peace at the provincial and national levels, and in other feminist activist work. My involvement in these movements and my education provided solace from the trauma of the military, but it always caught up with me.

There were many occasions for my military experience to resurface, such as my national coming out on CBC's *The Fifth Estate* with Hana

Gartner, my testimonial before the Royal Commission on Equality in Employment, or my participation in local and national media interviews. Every few years, someone would track me down and want me to comment on the military or on a social issue.

RETIREMENT AND CONTRADICTIONS

My involvement with the feminist peace movement was always a contradiction to my military background. When I was with the military, feminism was an issue. When I was with the feminist peace movement, my association with the military was an issue. The traditional patriarchal religions never worked for me, so I developed my own feminist spirituality. It does seem that my life has been one of many contradictions, and my life's mission has been to reconcile these opposing forces, internally and externally.

I did not, and could not, cut the military, religion, or feminism from my life. But it was time to retire. Since being diagnosed with cancer, the disease has sometimes taken centre stage; nonetheless, retirement has afforded me some contemplation, and I have chosen to live all of my contradictions in contemplation right here in Nova Scotia, where it all began. After all, one can never really get away from Nova Scotia, from this land, its culture, its people.

EPILOGUE

Throughout Wood's story runs a conversation filled with misunderstandings and resignations, but there is also resilience and wisdom. For over forty years, she fought vigorously against discrimination toward the lesbian and gay community by the military and the erasure of the role of women, and in particular lesbians, in social movements. Mostly, people only heard her voice as a whisper, and yet she was at the forefront of many battles.

Darl Wood has lived and embodied many contradictions in her life. Her religious background, her love of the military, her feminist peace work, her return to university, her spirituality, and her illness have all contributed to the unique and poignant narrative that is her life story.

Being Gay and Ex-Military in Nova Scotia

Frank Letourneau and Maya Eichler

PROLOGUE

This piece is based on an interview with Frank Letourneau conducted by Maya Eichler. Letourneau is a veteran of the Royal Canadian Navy currently residing in Halifax, NS. He served in the Canadian military from the late 1950s until 1970, at which point he was forced to resign from his position as navy lieutenant when confronted by military police with evidence of suspected homosexual behaviour. Letourneau's forced resignation was part of a systematic effort on the part of the federal government to detect and remove gays and lesbians from the public service. The LGBT Purge saw the targeting and investigation of "'suspected,' 'alleged,' and 'confirmed' homosexuals" (Kinsman and Gentile 2010, 3). Spanning from the late 1950s to the early 1990s, it was rooted in "the belief that gay men and lesbians suffered from a character weakness that made them vulnerable to blackmail and subversion, thus rendering them susceptible to the machinations of Soviet agents" (Kinsman and Gentile 2010, 3). Thousands of Canadians were affected by the Purge. Letourneau's story is one among many.

MAYA EICHLER: When did you join the Canadian military?

FRANK LETOURNEAU: It would have been the late '50s. I joined a program in Montreal at the Naval Reserve Unit. That was a three-year program for officer cadets. At the end of that, I was promoted to sub-lieutenant. I spent one more year doing that, and then transferred over to the Regular Force.

MAYA EICHLER: What made you join the forces originally?

FRANK LETOURNEAU: There was no military or naval tradition in my family, but I thought, I could start one. The navy was only happy to take me on because they hadn't spent a lot of money on me, unlike people who'd gone to military college, for example. I knew Halifax; I'd been here several times over the previous three or four years, so that was fine. I joined the ship, and things went well. Early on, I was awarded the watchkeeping certificate, which meant that I was responsible enough to take control of the ship during the four-hour watch.

MAYA EICHLER: It sounds like you enjoyed military life?

FRANK LETOURNEAU: Yes, and I had a captain who was supportive. I was told that I would be promoted to lieutenant when I turned twenty-three, after a couple of years' service. I was promoted as scheduled, and a few weeks after I got my promotion, I joined a new ship that had finished being built here in Halifax: HMCS *Annapolis*. The captain told me that he had put my name forward to be considered as the admiral's aide—the flag lieutenant, the position was called. I was completely surprised by this—I had no expectation. So, I went to the admiral's office the next day. I was interviewed, and I was offered the job.

MAYA EICHLER: How was that experience of being the admiral's aide?

FRANK LETOURNEAU: I spent almost two years as the admiral's aide, which was a very prestigious position. I enjoyed it a lot. The people I worked for, the admiral and his wife, were really nice people, and I became, for all intents and purposes, a member of their family. I dated their daughter, I chummed with their sons. At the end of my assignment as the admiral's aide, I had a choice of my next posting. I went on a long operations course. It was a one-year specializing course, and after that, I went back to sea as an operations officer for almost four years. And that's when I—you know, was ticking off all the boxes—was getting qualified for promotions to the next rank, lieutenant commander. My next job would have been probably a shore position, staff training, and then I would have gone back to sea as a second-in-command of a destroyer. So my career looked laid out, in a sort of very positive and interesting way.

MAYA EICHLER: But your career was cut short?

FRANK LETOURNEAU: Well, it came to a sudden standstill when the military police caught up with me.

MAYA EICHLER: And had you been set up for that or had someone given your name?

FRANK LETOURNEAU: Well, it took me a while to figure out how that happened. There were a couple of ways it could have happened. Because I had a high-level top-secret security clearance, my clearance was reviewed every two years. You had to fill out a form of people you spent time with and so on; it was fairly detailed. We assumed that the RCMP investigated. So, whenever I filled out one of these forms I thought, *you know, this could be trouble*—but it wasn't, as it turned out.

Surprisingly, I escaped detection in the course of those top-secret security clearance investigations. But I had met a guy who presented himself as a naval photographer—there was such a trade in the navy. And, yeah, so he had lots of pictures. He was a naval seaman, and I was an officer. So, we got together a few times—ah, that didn't end well; we broke up. I really didn't want to see him anymore. Now, he came knocking at my door a few times, but what happened is that, when I was called in, the information that they had on me could have only come from one source—that person. And what had happened, I learned this afterwards, is that he was not in the navy at all; he was a civilian employee on the base, and he was caught in this men's barracks—it was called *A Block* at the time—in a very compromising situation with a sailor. So the military police put the fear of God in him, even though they had no jurisdiction over him, and used their sort of classic trick: "Well, we'll go easy on you if you help us out here, and we're looking for names." Well, through him, they got my name and that of one other person that I know of. I never really had the chance, or the desire, to confront him about this, but this was clearly where they got enough information to start watching me, and they watched me for a year. By the time they called me in, they had a file on me that was really thick, and had a lot of information about people I'd gone out with—all the details, including pictures of my car on Citadel Hill, which was a very notorious cruising area back then.

So that's how they caught up with me, but they would have caught up with me eventually. Inevitably, I was going to be in a more visible situation as I became second-in-command of a ship. Now, I think, when the navy ran this business of security clearances and so on, there might have been a little more flexibility. In fact, I know of one situation where someone who had command of a ship was gay—but he got married. He was two ranks above me, and I was a lieutenant, but we talked a few times, and never really came out totally to each other, but I said, "So, you got married?" And he said, "I didn't have much choice, did I?"

MAYA EICHLER: What did you do next?

FRANK LETOURNEAU: At that stage, I really didn't know what to do with myself, but staying in Halifax seemed to be the obvious place to start because I had made some connections in Halifax, especially as the admiral's aide. I thought that this would be fine for a few years, but I would probably end up moving back to Montreal, Toronto, or Ottawa. But no, that never happened, and I just remained here. I bought a property downtown; I was in a relationship for seventeen years and made friends here. So, at various points when there might have been an option for me to move on and head back to central Canada, I chose to stay here.

MAYA EICHLER: Do you miss military life?

FRANK LETOURNEAU: I did at first, of course. The office I occupied as a civilian employee overlooked Halifax Harbour, and I could see ships come and go, and eventually, I would have had command over one of these ships. But you know, at the same time, the military was going through a rough patch: budgets had been cut back; ships were being decommissioned ahead of schedule; unification had come along that brought chaos into the three services. It was not a bad time to have left the navy, as it turned out.

MAYA EICHLER: So, you've left the military behind and transitioned to civilian life?

FRANK LETOURNEAU: Oh, totally. Undoubtedly. It depends a little bit on the timing, too. In my case, it happened in 1970. That's a long time ago. People were being forced out of the forces for another twenty years after that. So, people who were among the last ones to be forced out probably have more vivid memories, depending on what they faced on their way out. In my case, again, the transition was painless. In a sense, I was relieved that I no longer had to look over my shoulder. And the work I ended up doing was well-rewarded and interesting. Certainly, I made friends within the gay community. I just got on with my life. If I had somehow survived the Purge—and some people did, I know two people who somehow got away with being gay in the forces—if I had survived the Purge, to have led a double life for another twenty years, I can't imagine how that would have worked out. What, to get married just for show? And some people did that. What my departure from the navy accomplished is it allowed me to get on with a lifestyle that was no longer cause for disciplinary action.

MAYA EICHLER: What was it like to be gay in Nova Scotia in the '70s?

FRANK LETOURNEAU: It was the sexual revolution. Eventually there was a gay bar to go to. The cruising areas were very active. Meeting people was easy, you know. If you were just looking for hookups, that was easily accomplished, and along the way you made friends. You slept with one, and then you became friends. And there were parties.

MAYA EICHLER: Do you feel more connected to the LGBTQ+ community or the veteran community?

FRANK LETOURNEAU: To a much larger degree, it's the LGBTQ+ community. Veterans...no, I've not had any serious connections with. I attend the November 11 Remembrance Day ceremonies, but other than that, I have never really thought of joining the Royal Canadian Legion or being actively involved in any other kind of veteran organization. It just hasn't occurred to me—and possibly because of some lingering bitterness about the fact that I was forced out of the military. And also, I wondered to what extent I would be well received by my fellow veterans, because I think eventually word got out that, you know, *Frank Letourneau resigned his commission alright—but he had no choice; he was found out to be gay,* and back then it wasn't allowed. So perhaps for that reason, I was less inclined to look for contacts within the veteran community.

MAYA EICHLER: And in terms of the gay veteran community? You've talked about how you have not really sought out that community.

FRANK LETOURNEAU: I wouldn't have even known how to do that.

MAYA EICHLER: Or ex-military folks? Considering that you were in for ten years, military folks would have been such a huge part of your socialization and your social connections, no?

FRANK LETOURNEAU: Yes, but it ended. It ended so abruptly. I have no reason to seek connections with these people, you know. If I ran into some of them by accident, I'd be happy to chat. So no, I had no desire.

MAYA EICHLER: Your identity is no longer connected to the military in any way?

FRANK LETOURNEAU: No, not at all.

MAYA EICHLER: And when you talk to people, do you ever mention that you were in the military? Like if you introduce yourself to someone.

FRANK LETOURNEAU: Oh, I will, if the opportunity presents itself. I will mention the fact that I was in the navy, but that's it. Now if they start asking questions about that, I'll say, I was in the navy until I was not allowed to stay in the navy any longer. But that kind of conversation is rare. So no, I've had no desire to stay in touch. And the other thing is that people who serve in the navy move on and move around, and mostly, they're all straight, they're married, have kids. Their life is very different from mine.

MAYA EICHLER: How did you feel about the prime minister's apology to LGBTQ2 military members and public servants who faced persecution and discrimination? You were at the apology ceremony, weren't you?

FRANK LETOURNEAU: I was there, and I watched the prime minister stand in the House of Commons and deliver the apology in a very moving way. Afterwards, I met with him and several senior members of the Canadian military who all thanked me for my service. So, that was quite an experience. I was deeply moved by that. But you know, life goes on. Six years ago, I would have never imagined anything like this happening.

MAYA EICHLER: Thank you for sharing your story with me.

EPILOGUE

In 2018, Frank Letourneau gave the following address at the Halifax Pride parade:

Good evening. I served as an officer in the Canadian navy from the late 1950s to January 1970. At that point, I was the operations officer and a department head on the destroyer HMCS Saguenay. *However, my career came to a sudden stop when I was summoned by the military police and presented with information which they had gathered for about one year and which strongly suggested that I was gay. Rather than deny it and face a humiliating transfer from my ship to an insignificant posting ashore and the downgrading of my top-secret security clearance, I saw no alternative but to resign my commission and bring to an abrupt end what had every sign of being a successful career with promotions to higher rank.*

As shocking as this was, it was far more gentle and manageable than what a friend of mine went through about twenty years later as an enlisted member of the same ship I had served on, HMCS Saguenay. *In his case, an ordinary seaman still in his late teens confided in the ship's medic that he was brutally beaten up by some of his shipmates. He and the others were sentenced to one week in detention, but the captain said it was for his own protection. It gets worse: he was taken off the ship and left in some kind of limbo for a few months on the naval base, but, along the way, a never-identified naval person phoned his mother and informed her that her son was facing a dishonourable discharge for misconduct. This severely shook up his parents so much that his mother attempted suicide and remained incapacitated until the end of her life. He was released from the forces but had the good fortune of being befriended and encouraged by his landlady when he resumed his education. He and I managed to get our lives back together, but sadly many did not.*

This is the kind of waste and distress caused by a policy which the Canadian Forces continued to pursue for over twenty years against the law of the land and until they were faced with losing in court in 1992.

Thank you!

Chapter 2

Military Families

Introduction

Leigh Spanner

Canada's military is made up of men and women in uniform who serve and sacrifice for the country. This is the public face of the military. In private, most military members have families whose support and contributions are essential to the members' ability to serve. The Canadian Armed Forces call military families "the strength behind the uniform" to signal their critical role. But, like the adage suggests, the stories of military families are often relegated to the background, spotlighting instead the chronicles of those who officially serve. Telling these stories reveals the extent to which armed forces rely on the work and commitment of families in order to function. These stories also challenge conventional notions of what constitutes a family. The accounts of military families lay bare the far-reaching and complex consequences of being prepared for and engaged in the conduct of war. Spouses are often called on to provide care for injured military members and sometimes experience vicarious or secondary trauma themselves. Children of military members experience long separations from their service parents and have to get creative about staying in touch. But military families find a source of comfort and support in one another, forming a strong community and creating a deep sense of solidarity. This is true in Nova Scotia in particular, where military families are very much part of the fabric of our society.

While the military is a public institution, family and home life are normally understood as private and sacred. This conceptual dichotomy makes less visible the experiences of military families and dilutes the key role they play in supporting an operationally effective and sustainable military force. Because love and intimacy are associated with family life, the contributions of military families are taken for granted and assumed to take place naturally. Consequently, the tales of military families often go untold. Their stories are diverse and sometimes contradictory, ranging from sentiments of pride, loyalty, resilience, perseverance, adventure, and empowerment to sacrifice, resentment, betrayal, and grief. Yet, the demands placed on military families are profound and their sacrifices are beyond compare: frequent relocation, recurrent and prolonged separation from the service member, and management of the risks and consequences of having a loved one in the military.

When military families do feature in popular narratives, they are often framed as displaying pride and loyalty to the members of the military through grief and loss. For example, one of the most widely depicted images of military families is the accolade of the Silver Cross Mother, awarded by the Royal Canadian Legion on Remembrance Day. The Silver Cross Mother represents widows and mothers of Canadian sailors, aviators, and soldiers. The 2002 and 2003 Silver Cross accolades were given to Doreen Coolen of Hubbards, NS, and Charlotte Lynn Smith of Tatamagouche, NS. Both women lost their sons to friendly fire while they were deployed in Afghanistan. Nova Scotia and its military families paid an especially high toll during the war in Afghanistan. While the province accounts for 3 percent of Canada's population, 10 percent of Canadian Armed Forces members killed in Afghanistan were from Nova Scotia.[1] Likewise, military families feature prominently in media coverage of deployment-related injuries such as PTSD, veteran suicides, the Highway of Heroes processions, or the events of the Red Fridays Foundation of Canada. These accounts feature war-related loss, mostly of military wives and mothers, whose suffering must not be in vain. But this is only a fraction of the story.

Military families experience war and peace in far more expansive and complex ways than through grief and loss. By listening to their stories, we learn a bit more about what everyday life in times of war and peace looks like: of the inevitable flooding of basements, broken-down washing machines, and sick children on the first weeks of a deployment; of the sadness at the empty place at the dinner table and missed anniversaries; of the stress, and perhaps excitement, of having to purchase a home within five days to accommodate a new posting. Their accounts give us insights into military marriages, such as renegotiating household dynamics when the member returns after months of being away; birthing a child or losing a pregnancy while a spouse is deployed; and managing careers, whether that's giving up a job for a new posting or finding ways to maintain employment as a military spouse. We grasp an appreciation for the military child, who grows up quickly and might be unfamiliar with their parent after they return from a deployment, who gets a second story at bedtime to offset the separation from their parent, who eats pizza more often than is ideal, and who might one day enlist, generating a perplexing blend of pride and regret in their parents. Stories of military families acknowledge the military caregiver and the nurture, burnout, frustration, and empowerment involved in supporting a loved one who was injured in service. And we gain an appreciation for the solidarity and love that is shared between fellow military families and spouses, and the cohesive community that results.

Service life requires military members and their families to be displaced from broader chosen and biological family networks. Military families move three times more frequently than civilian families, have "little input over where they are posted, when they are posted, and for how long" and identify this operational requirement as the most unsettling feature of military life (Daigle 2013, 4). To offset the isolation and the challenges of military life, members of military families often feel a sense of solidarity with and obligation to support one another like family. That the Canadian military "is one big family" and "takes care of its own" are common turns of phrase. Taking care of one another like family can look like sharing holidays together, being available for emergency childcare assistance, picking up household items such as food and diapers for other families, providing emotional support and comfort to one another during trying times, connecting spouses and families to the community, and grieving together over the loss of a fellow community member, even if the deceased was not known personally. The activities and relationships in the military community challenge conventional ideas about who constitutes a family because kinship and support transcend the nuclear family. A fellow military wife might be more like a sister or a mother, the military kids down the street might be more like cousins to your kids, and the member who lost their life in service might feel like kin. The stories of military families embrace a wider understanding of *family*, one that is not reduced to blood ties.

Importantly, attending to the stories of military families, in all their versions, centres the experiences and work of those not typically featured in accounts of the armed forces—women. Despite growing diversity in the Canadian military, which includes an increasing number of servicewomen, and in Canadian families, which are less and less likely to take the nuclear form, women constitute 98 percent of military spouses (CFMWS 2019, 7). Thus, the stories of "the strength behind the uniform" are women's stories. They tell of the work that is required to foster a family and a home life that are conducive to military service. As we call attention to stories of military families, we recognize the contributions of women and the work done by them.

In this chapter, we highlight the story of a military wife and the work she does to support her family and her husband's career. Catherine Littler, who is originally from Cape Breton and whose husband is posted to Halifax, discusses becoming a parent and navigating her education and career while living a military life. Despite the centrality of women in military families, the face of military families in Canada is undergoing change. As the makeup of the Canadian Armed Forces continues to modernize through the increased recruitment of women, visible minorities, and 2SLGBTQIA+ service members, so does our understanding of the military family. Research on military families is crucial in tracking these changes. The value of military family research is outlined in Deborah Norris's reflections on her thirty-year journey as a military family investigator. Systematic analysis of the composition, practices, needs, and challenges of military families is crucial in providing them with institutional support such as programming at Military Family Resource Centres.

These two stories offer a more comprehensive understanding of the impact of the military on Nova Scotian families, including on the work that military families are obliged to do and on their commitment to relationships, communities, and the armed forces.

NOTES

1 Of the 158 Canadian Armed Forces members who were killed in Afghanistan, 15 were from Nova Scotia.

I Knew What I Was Getting Into, Right? Reflections from a Military Spouse

Catherine Littler

Growing up on Cape Breton Island, I had little exposure to military life. My own impressions were limited to popular films, which focused primarily on US military experiences. The picture etched in my mind was of men who were of elite physical fitness and had a masculine mystique. These men were often divorced or, at the very least, struggling in their personal relationships. This seemed common, but well worth the sacrifice when compared to the national duty to uphold their country's security, freedom, and dignity. As the years passed, I had the opportunity to educate myself more about socially prescribed gender roles and identities. The more I learned, the more I took issue with my image of a typical military man.

I met my husband, Mark, in January 2011 in Halifax, NS. I was twenty; he was twenty-five and had been in the military for about seven years. I had always told myself I would never settle down with a first responder, military or otherwise. Mark and I casually dated for the remainder of 2011. In the spring of 2012, Mark was loaded onto the Royal Canadian Navy course for clearance divers at Fleet Diving Unit—Pacific, and we made the move to our new home for the next year. At the time, I thought it was the most challenging year of our life together. Looking back ten years and countless deployments later, I sometimes long for the days when Mark was on that course. At the very least, he was home. Our life was hectic; he was constantly exhausted, both mentally and physically, and although I was experiencing struggles of my own, they did not compare to those my boyfriend was facing. And besides, our life would be "normal" once this course was over, right?

Every year has been different, but also the same. Every deployment feels like it will never end, but eventually it does. And in an almost poetic manner, all of these events blend together to form a blurred compilation of memories that look the same. After a few years, I began to realize that our life wasn't going to start once he finished a course, got back from a deployment, or finally got the posting message we were waiting for. This *was* our life. I needed to either extinguish this idea entirely, start looking at our life differently and embrace its uniqueness, or get out. Mark and I had a healthy and loving relationship, so the decision was not a difficult one to make.

After this realization, I tried on many hats in the attempt to make this foreign role fit. And foreign is exactly what it was. After all, I was from Cape Breton. I had a large family who lived close to each other. The women were dedicated to their roles as mothers and wives, and the men worked hard in labour occupations. No one left; life was predictable to say the least, and I took comfort in this predictability. The divide between the genders was very clear and prescribed. My mother knew how to be a wife and a mother because she was fulfilling a role similar to that of her mother and grandmother before her. Being a military wife was something I had never observed, and I had absolutely no idea how to be one.

In an attempt to fit into the military mould, I first looked to media. What did these women look like? Supporters! *I can do that,* I thought. Whatever he needs, that is what I'll be. I put my personal career goals and other dreams aside because that seemed to me what military spouses did. These women were dedicated to the cause entirely. The men went away, and the women held down the fort, so to speak. Never did I see a military spouse who was also a CEO, a professor, or anything other than a wife and mother. These women did precarious tasks, sometimes held jobs that were perceived as difficult and undesirable, and were often emotionally tormented. But this was expected. At the time, I had not begun my university education and was working as a waitress. I believed that Mark's job was more prestigious and important than mine, and more mentally and physically challenging. Therefore, my main job should be to support him. For the next four years, I followed Mark through his career, supporting him completely. In the beginning, I convinced myself that it was enough, and my identity could be fulfilled through this role alone. Eventually though, it was not. Although I have always aspired to be a wife and mother who kept a clean home, an organized schedule, and nutritious meals on the table, I have also always wanted to be a scholar. However, I thought these two lives could never coexist. So, I chose the one that was most important to me.

During two particular years within this time period, I lost my grandmother, a critical person in my life, and was deeply affected by three miscarriages, one of which almost claimed my own life. In these losses, I felt alone. Although they were Mark's children too, he was not with me for any of the miscarriages. Mark appeared emotionally unaffected, which was not the case, but because of the disconnect, it felt that way to me. Rather than bringing us closer together, these tragedies led me to begin to resent him and his job. Along with being away from Mark, I had no support system of my own. I spent all these years building a solid support system for Mark and I forgot, or simply chose to ignore, myself. I became depressed in my solitude and began to struggle to find meaning in my life. What was the point of all of these sacrifices if the one I was sacrificing for was never here when I needed him most? Mark is a great man and a wonderful supporter but, because of my own notions of what a military relationship should look like, I never gave him the opportunity to show me that.

I appeared strong and unaffected in front of him through these losses because I did not want my grief to affect him in his job. Mark works with explosives, dives under pressure, and is often put in high-stress situations. I thought that if I were to show what I thought was weakness, I could be putting him in danger. These experiences, although damaging, have also made me a resilient person. This is a quality that I am tremendously grateful for and that has continued to help me in many areas of my life. I began to feel oppressed and voiceless in the subordinate role I had assigned myself and decided I'd had enough. I realized I was not made to be a "yes" woman and that there were important goals and voices inside me that were essential to my full identity. And if I had to be my only advocate in this isolated life, then so be it. I became a health coach and personal trainer and realized I had a true passion for food, education, and social policy. Once my frame of mind shifted, I became inspired by my experiences as a military wife. I wouldn't live as a second-class citizen in my own marriage, in my own life, anymore. I wouldn't allow the title of *military spouse* to be the only role defining me.

In the fall of 2015, I enrolled at Mount Saint Vincent University and began studying for a bachelor of science in applied human nutrition, which I received in May of 2019. I have since completed a master of science in applied human nutrition and am now entering the PhD in health at Dalhousie University. When I enrolled in my bachelor's program in the fall of 2015, I was also pregnant with our first child, Hannah. She was born six weeks prematurely in February 2016. During my hospitalization beginning in early February, I continued my full-time studies from a hospital bed and eventually from the NICU at the IWK Health Centre. I thought that life could not possibly get any harder than it was at that moment. I was a new student in a difficult program, a new mother terrified of losing her child, and a military wife who was now worried that if I lost my husband because of his job, I would also be losing the father of my child. My breast milk never came in after four months of struggle, which was a devastating reality for me as a nutrition student, breastfeeding advocate, and mother. And I still had final exams and papers pending completion. I was a complete mess. Regardless, I had my precious daughter who is now six years old and perfectly healthy. Another wonderful and healthy child, Dylan, was born in May 2017.

In March 2018, any previous notions I had of the word *difficult* were radically shaken. Mark was deployed until mid-April; we essentially had no immediate support system; I was taking a full course load, and the Canadian winter was in full swing. What could possibly go wrong? Fourteen days into this deployment tested all the perseverance and resilience I had acquired. Shortly after my husband left home, both of our children became ill with an awful gastrointestinal flu. I wrote to my professors and luckily was able to be excused from classes and extend several deadlines. Before I knew it, those deadlines were upon me; exams were days away, and my children were still vomiting. The days blended together as I tended to my sick toddlers and struggled with tasks many people take for granted. I know I certainly did. How does one shop for groceries, shovel the driveway, or finish a paper with two sick kids? The answer became evident: you don't.

Days into my children's flu, a winter storm hit. We lost power, we had no food or formula and no way to wash any of the vomit-covered blankets. I remember sitting in my daughter's single bed in the middle of the night with no power, a sick baby on either side of me, wrapped in every blanket we owned to keep warm, covered in vomit, listening to the storm. At first, I felt like a complete failure, but then I began to feel pride. There I was, smack-dab in the middle of complete chaos, and we were okay. I was figuring it out, alone. My tears turned to laughter, and I felt a surge of self-confidence. It was an experience I would never have had if I had not been a military wife. My bitterness and resentment toward Mark's job started to look more like thankfulness and humility. My children got better. I finished the semester with A's. And I gained a new appreciation and respect for myself and my husband, which has brought us closer.

In my experience, military spouses are all too often put on the back burner. After all, we knew what we were getting into, right? At least, this might be what we tell ourselves. The truth is that I didn't realize what being a military spouse truly involved, and I don't think many of us do. It has been my experience that the struggles faced by military spouses are often devalued, discredited, and taken for granted. Our hardships are seen as luxuries compared to those of our spouses. The simple reality is that regardless of my spouse's job, we are in a marriage, not just part of a military machine. We both deserve to be cared for and recognized. I am not just an extension of the military or a clearance diver's support system, maid, chef, and nanny. My life's purpose is not to make excuses for shortcomings or injustices in my marriage by saying, "I knew what I was getting into." What I knew I was getting into was a marriage, a partnership with Mark. Yes, I knew what his job was. Yes, I knew he would be away from home. Yes, I knew he would be in dangerous situations. But not once did I consider that being a wife of a military member would mean that I would have to swallow my voice.

If I have learned nothing else as a military spouse, I've learned that, first, military spouses are resilient and gritty. Second, although we have a crucial role to play in our spouses' job performance, it does not fully define us. As military spouses, we should not wait for our partners' deployment to end before we work on what is important to us. For me, that was many things, including my health, career, and social life. Third, while I still firmly believe that our society projects military men as the picture of strength and a focal point of their families, I now understand that these men are able to maintain these personas due to strong support systems, which in our case is a supporting wife. Also, many military men struggle with these forced identities and values. I believe it is crucial for the health of military families and military members to begin breaking down toxic masculine values and to start exploring mental health and diversity within the forces.

In the end, I am a military wife among many other things. I take great pride in my identity and my respect and love for my husband, and I have a better understanding of my role in my marriage and of the military. As military spouses, we have a unique role in supporting our significant others so that they are equipped to serve our country. It is challenging, emotional, and may seem fruitless at times; it requires selflessness and perseverance, but our lives are also filled with pride, a strong sense of community, and the understanding that we are part of something much larger than ourselves. I am grateful for my experiences and believe that I am stronger for them. I look forward to the next years of our marriage and to advancements in the quality of education and support available for our troops and their families.

Never in a Straight Line but Always in the Right Direction: The Story of a Military Family Researcher

Deborah Norris

In the late 1980s, a young, enthusiastic-but-inexperienced academic with a master of science degree in family studies, newly hired at Mount Saint Vincent University (MSVU), walked up the steps of an imposing old building on Gottingen Street in Halifax and through the door. That door turned out to be a portal to a rewarding career as a military family researcher—a career that has spanned three decades to date. This career path has never followed a straight line, and roadblocks and dead ends have emerged occasionally, but it has always gone in the right direction.

So, what led me to walk through that door? My story began with a keen interest in work–family balance that I developed during my graduate program in family studies at the University of Alberta. This interest was sparked, in part, by the faculty who taught me there and, in part, by my personal history. My father was a banker and was transferred around Atlantic Canada many times in my childhood, a practice not uncommon in banking at that time. When we lived in Halifax, the headquarters of Canada's east coast navy and home to many serving members and their families, I was described by my teachers as a "bank brat," often sitting in classrooms next to other students identified as "navy brats" or "air force brats."

Throughout my childhood, my parents encouraged me and my sisters to see the benefits of our experiences as a bank family. They tried to see the benefits, too, but looking back, I can recall times when maintaining a positive attitude was difficult, and for good reason. What got us through those times was the informal support we received from fellow bank families and from a large extended family who provided us with refuge each summer when we went "home" to Prince Edward Island, the province where my parents had been born and raised. There were no formal work–family programs available to help us and other bank families.

Fast-forward to my early career as a faculty member at MSVU. I was finding my way, teaching courses in family studies, and developing a research program. The interdependence between work and family remained at the top of my list of possible research pursuits, with workplace programs and policies to support the families of workers evolving as a related interest. So, when I serendipitously heard about a new family support centre to be established at CFB Halifax, this bank brat was intrigued. I had to find out more. Somehow, I found the name of a contact person on the base, cold-called them, declared my interest in work–family programming, and audaciously offered to help them develop some programs. To my surprise, my offer was accepted and that led me to walk through the door of that old building on Gottingen Street.

Within a couple of months of that first telephone call, I developed three programs emphasizing education, support, and prevention for the new Military Family Support Centre. (The name of the centre was eventually changed to the Military Family Resource Centre because of concerns that *support* implied that families participating in centre programs were in crisis and required therapeutic intervention, not preventative support, which was the mandate of the centre.) In consultation with the centre staff, I developed two parenting programs and a program for military spouses. Shortly thereafter, I facilitated these programs for growing groups of military members and their families. Over time, I involved my family studies students at MSVU in the programming. My graduate students, cooperative education students, and practicum students often co-facilitated the programs, participated in program redevelopment, and developed new programs. Some of those students were later hired as full-time employees at the centre and are still working there.

As it turns out, developing the centre at CFB Halifax was an integral step in implementing an initiative led by the Department of National Defence (DND) in 1987—the Family Support Program Project. The project was developed in response to ongoing advocacy efforts by a group of military spouses in Alberta, the Organizational Society of Spouses of Military Members (OSSOMM—pronounced "awesome"). From these first steps, the Military Family Services Program was launched in 1991, culminating in a network of not-for-profit, arms-length Military Family Resource Centres established at bases, wings, and support units across the country.

Circling back to the late 1980s, as a young academic, I was planning to pursue a PhD program but uncertain about the focus. Again, serendipity stepped in. While on a coffee break during a program for military spouses I was facilitating at the new CFB Halifax Military Family Support Centre, I overheard a participant commiserating with a fellow participant who, like her, was anticipating the imminent six-month deployment of her husband. She casually remarked, "Well, here we go again. We have got to work them out and work them in."

That remark stayed with me. At the time, I was beginning to read the work of feminist sociologist Dorothy Smith. Smith asserts that institutional practices are accomplished through the work ongoing in everyday lives. I began to wonder if the work to be enacted by the military spouses in my program was linked to the work of the military institution. Still curious about this, within a year, I had enrolled in a PhD program in education at Dalhousie University where I had the opportunity to be mentored by faculty who had studied with Smith at the Ontario Institute for Studies in Education at the University of Toronto. My doctoral research was an institutional ethnography, a method developed by Smith, and my dissertation was entitled "Working Them Out...Working Them In: The Everyday Lives of

Female Military Partners Experiencing the Cycle of Deployment." I will always be grateful to the military spouse in that program for her offhand remark.

In the years that have followed, my passion for military family research has intensified. For the first ten years following the completion of my PhD research, encouraged by Deborah Harrison, a sociologist at the University of New Brunswick and a well-established Canadian military family researcher, I enjoyed a collaborative working relationship with military defence scientists at the Directorate of Quality of Life at DND. We worked together on a number of projects focusing on military families. The questions guiding this work centred on the relationship between military family functioning and the priorities of the military institution. The results of this military defence research often influenced the development of military family policies and programs, particularly those implemented through the network of Military Family Resource Centres across the country. For example, a study examining the impact of deployments on military families yielded evidence supporting deployment programs facilitated at the centres. Over time, the boundaries of my research with this team expanded to include issues related to health and caregiving in the military context. One study undertaken with a graduate student brought into view a problem "hiding in plain sight" within the military institution: the dilemma faced by female serving members who are parents and who are required to be absent from their families through deployments and other operations. A study that invited military single parents to share their challenges was also implemented, involving focus groups conducted across the country. From this, an interest in military family resilience evolved, a focus that remains integral to my current research program.

An unexpected turn in the road in 2006 interrupted my military family research activity for a time. Mandated by the new federal government elected that year, all DND research from then on was to be conducted by internal defence scientists only, a practice that continued for several years. While this temporary hiatus was disappointing, my interest in military families remained as strong as ever. I developed and taught a course at MSVU focusing on military families. I continued to support the work ongoing at the CFB Halifax Military Family Resource Centre. And new research questions were emerging. Canadian Armed Forces personnel were now serving in combat missions, a new role they had increasingly taken on since the Gulf War. The impact of operational stress injuries incurred in combat, particularly PTSD, on the families of serving members and veterans became my newest area of interest. While researchers in other countries, particularly the US, were investigating PTSD in serving members and veterans and its impacts on their families, very little was happening in Canada.

In 2010, following a few years where I struggled to maintain momentum as a military family researcher, I received notice that a conference focusing on the health of members of the armed forces and veterans was to be held in Kingston, ON. I was, of course, intrigued, and invited my graduate student who had just completed a qualitative study focusing on secondary trauma in veteran spouses to submit an abstract. She and I attended the conference together, and her paper was well-received, prompting conference organizers to mention to me, "You know, we should be doing more research on military families in Canada." I didn't need to be convinced.

That small conference held in 2010 grew into a group now known as the Canadian Institute for Military and Veteran Health Research, a hub for military, veteran, and family research in Canada. This development was a game-changer for me, the impetus for the development of rich and rewarding collaborations with fellow researchers focusing on military and veteran families both in Canada and abroad. The research we do is applied. It has informed policy and program development at Veterans Affairs Canada and DND. This has given me great satisfaction, considering that everything I have done and everything I will continue to do as a military family researcher has been shaped by what I learned through the experience of facilitating programs for serving members and their families at the beginning of my career. My research road appears to be straighter now than it was at the beginning. The way forward seems more certain, illuminated by a brighter light of interest in the health and well-being of military and veteran families in Canada. Best of all, fellow researchers now walk the road too.

Chapter 3

Refugee Communities

Introduction

Catherine Baillie Abidi

The number of people forcibly displaced because of persecution, violence, or violations of human rights has risen year after year at alarming rates. More than eighty-two million people were forced to migrate in 2020, half of whom were under the age of eighteen (UNHCR 2021). The magnitude of this humanitarian crisis is unprecedented. And yet, the way the international community tells stories about migration related to armed conflict consistently fails to meaningfully analyze the root causes that force masses to move. The international migration narratives also fail to include the voices of those directly affected, leaving large gaps in our understanding of the impacts of war and the potential for peace.

Despite growing humanitarian crises, including terror-related violence, and despite international commitments to prevent violence, discussion of forced migration is increasingly set within an anti-refugee narrative (Institute for Economics & Peace 2020). This narrative associates migration with criminality and security concerns, resulting in the fear of the "dangerous other." This growing conservative, nationalistic, and exclusionary political view is now driving the story of the "dangerous refugee," which is growing in all corners of the world and moving alarmingly toward a single story of protection *from* refugees as opposed to *of* refugees. Socialized norms of distrust toward the "other" contribute to deepening public acceptance of the "dangerous refugee," and the impacts result in exclusionary migration policies and reduced protections for refugees. Given this context, we must counter the story of the "dangerous other" and create spaces for stories of resilience, inclusive communities, and the value of diversity. We need to better understand how storytelling can facilitate social transformations to shift away from the present-day narrative of "dangerous other" toward respect for a shared and collective humanity.

STORYTELLING FOR SOCIAL CHANGE

Storytelling is perhaps the oldest teaching method and one that is common across regions and cultures. We tell stories to remember people and events; we tell stories to entertain; we tell stories to build community; and we tell stories to challenge myths or social norms. Unfortunately, the story of the "dangerous refugee" persists. Refugee voices are absent in the storytelling, and counter-narratives addressing the resiliency of those forced to flee and the collective humanity operating during this unprecedented time are underrepresented. Diverse stories that challenge the "dangerous other" provide an opportunity to humanize the experiences of people fleeing humanitarian crises and to transform anti-refugee policies and practices.

Two storytelling initiatives in Nova Scotia—the Invisible Women, Concrete Barriers network and the speaker series A Story to Tell and a Place for the Telling—offer examples of how counter-narratives can emerge to critique and transform harmful representations of forced migration. This introduction explores the tensions and lessons learned from engaging in storytelling within such globally focused community projects.

That refugee voices are underrepresented in the global narrative on forced migration is concerning; that women's voices are omitted is alarming. To create opportunities to share stories and create change *with* women refugees, multiple social justice-oriented organizations in the Halifax area started a network called Invisible Women, Concrete Barriers (IWCB). The IWCB network was created to identify and subsequently reduce barriers faced by women refugees in Nova Scotia (Baillie Abidi 2008). The work of the IWCB network was inspired by the stories of the women participants who were forced to leave their countries of origin. Over several discussions, the women participants identified barriers such as lack of access to education and employment, challenges seeking medical and health services, and stigma related to how they arrived in Canada. Together, the non-governmental partners and the women participants created case studies and briefings and hosted workshops with policy-makers to elevate their voices and to seek change to restrictive policies and practices. As a result, the Government of Nova Scotia adopted new polices relating to refugee healthcare and education, and the policy-makers who engaged with the women refugees identified the importance of hearing stories directly in order to enhance their perspective of the complexities of war and forced migration.

A place for the telling

A key lesson learned from the IWCB network was the lack of safe spaces for marginalized communities, and particularly marginalized women, to share their experiences. To create safe spaces, the IWCB network partnered with the Halifax Public Libraries to create a public education series on forced migration. A Story to Tell and a Place for the Telling was a program designed by the Canadian Red Cross to create a safe space for refugees to tell stories and to engage with other community members. The IWCB network embraced this approach and selected a series of topics based on current events and contemporary debates, hosting five events a year over a five-year period. For example, one speaker series focused on forced migration and detention for individuals coming from conflict-affected countries. Another speaker series demonstrated the toll that armed conflict and forced migration has on children and their families as they navigate safe passages. A key feature of A Story to Tell was the inclusion of first-person storytellers and, with that, preparing the storyteller to share personal accounts in a public setting. The results of this program included hundreds of Nova Scotians indicating that first-person stories challenged their understanding of peace and conflict, citizenship, and precarious statuses and increased their understanding of the humanness of forced migration. A Story to Tell also provided an opportunity for community members with refugee backgrounds to raise their voices and fill gaps in the stories.

FORCED-MIGRATION PERSPECTIVES

This chapter focuses on the experiences and reflections of four individuals who were forced to flee their homes due to violence, political persecution, or war. Sharing stories from within refugee communities can challenge the homogenous narrative of the "dangerous other." People forced to migrate share a common bond in their connection to experiences of persecution, violence, and precarious journeys. However, refugees are a highly heterogeneous group and their life stories are diverse, influenced by space, time, and culture. Collaborating to create spaces for diverse stories to be told and creating the conditions for these stories to be heard are essential to challenging the narrative of the "dangerous refugee."

While the four contributors' experiences are unique, they share themes of human connection, perseverance, peace building, and hope for stronger communities. The chapter begins with reflections from Amara Bangura, an experienced journalist who has reported on violence and armed conflict all over the world. Bangura paints a complex picture of his own journey, reflecting on the impacts of war and the resilience and the leadership of women who sacrifice greatly to protect their communities. The second contribution is from Nareen Haj Ali, a lawyer, humanitarian, and mother of four. Ali shares a heartfelt account of her journey as a mother and the lengths she took to protect her children from harm. The next contribution is from Viyan Ali, Nareen Haj Ali's daughter, who captures her reflections as a child during the war in Syria. Viyan Ali's voice, like those of many other children affected by war, is often missing from stories of peace and war, so it was essential to include. The final entry is from Marianela Fuertes, an internationally acclaimed human rights lawyer who speaks to the realities and complexities of surviving a civil war that has been sustained across generations. Fuertes's story illustrates the bravery of those who seek social justice in the pursuit of a world where the human rights of everyone are respected.

The contributors chose to participate in this book to add their voices to narratives on forced migration, peace, and war and to ensure the complexities, the compassion, and the common humanity that exists within and beyond violence are shared with the broader community. We invite you to join us in this dialogue focused on building communities where respect for all is achieved and where inclusion, connection, and humanity are the quintessential core of a community.

Confronting the Past: Remembering Memuna

Amara Bangura

When you hear about war, what images come to mind? When I was young, I loved listening to international media. I particularly admired war correspondents who risked their lives to tell stories of civilians trapped in conflicts. I responded to most of those stories with mixed feelings. I often caught myself thinking: *Why do civilians stay in a war zone? Why don't they leave?* It never occurred to me that it might be a situation I would have to deal with in practical terms until the war broke out in my country, Sierra Leone, in 1991.

As far as I can still remember, there is no greater suffering imaginable than being a civilian in a deadly war zone. Your entire world shrinks, and you focus solely on survival, on finding moments of peace. In most cases, your life ambitions are dashed—often overshadowed by the everyday struggles to survive. With no prior military training, you have to adopt new skills of how to escape bullets and bombardment. We have all heard of refugees risking their lives to cross dangerous borders in search of safety, but they are mostly the lucky ones. They made it out of the war alive. Many others, however, stay and hold out in the war zones, and often nobody is there to protect them. They stay for various reasons: some are too old to leave the conflict, some have poor health or lack finances, and some are trapped by fighting forces in an area under constant bombardment.

I was a teenager when the war broke out. It started in the Kailahun District in the east of Sierra Leone, which shares a border with neighbouring Liberia. The Revolutionary United Front led by a former army corporal, Foday Sankoh, made Kailahun its base, and for many years, they would travel through the forests of Kailahun District to launch attacks, loot, and destroy homes in towns and villages across the country. After years of brutal fighting, the rebels finally made it to the north, and they made Makeni their base—the northern city where I grew up.

I lived in Makeni for most of the war, with occasional visits to other parts of the country. That experience was horrifying. In my everyday life, I witnessed a lot of atrocities that you could imagine in a war. Attacks and counterattacks by forces loyal to the government and infighting within rebel forces were the daily experience. Physical torture, looting, rape, and abductions were also common practices by all the fighting factions, including the government forces and the Economic Community of West African States Monitoring Group forces led by the Nigerian troops. Makeni, our once-beautiful city, became a dangerous place to live. The rule of law was replaced by the rule of the gun. Our traditional protective structures, including family and community networks, the judicial system, and the security sector, were all torn apart. The education and health systems were also quickly broken down, and the sick were either left to die or to turn to traditional medicine that most often included herbs. Pregnant women and children endured traumatic injuries as a result of heavy bombardment by rebel fighters and air raids by the government-supported Alpha Jet fleet. Living in a conflict zone, incidents like these were a fact of life and, more so, a part of life. Many families trapped in those difficult conditions had to make difficult decisions—to live with the rebel fighters or escape them and face the government militia groups (the Kamajors), who also unleashed terror on the civilians they were supposed to protect. But living through those difficult times also opened my eyes to another side of humanity that I have come to appreciate: the courage and strength of some women who took up the challenge to pick up the pieces, while others were busy bleeding the country.

Sierra Leone is largely a patriarchal society where men have always been at the forefront of decision-making in homes, communities, and even in national governance. But eleven years of war changed some of the dynamics and forced women into some unprecedented new roles. Whilst some were conscripted and became guerrilla fighters, some became bodyguards, and many others were at the forefront of peace-making. In fact, in 1995, women's groups throughout the country organized a public demonstration and a march that demanded an election process and led to a consultative conference for good governance. Similarly, in many smaller communities across the country, women took up leadership roles and became known as "mamy queens." They performed crucial duties such as organizing their towns and communities to map out strategies to respond to the rebel fighters who were high on drugs. They led negotiations with the rebels and pro-government forces to keep their towns and communities safe. Under difficult circumstances, many women relentlessly explored new opportunities to contribute to their families' survival, adapted previous livelihoods, and created new ones. In most families, not only were women left to shoulder the main household chores, but with most men being absent or unable to fulfill their traditional roles as breadwinners, women were also mostly responsible for providing the resources to cover basic family needs even in those difficult periods.

In 1999, the rebels had captured most of the districts and major towns in the country, and I was with relatives hiding on a farm in a small village called Konsho, about seven miles from Makeni. It was there that I met Memuna Bangura, a young woman who was also hiding there with her family. She and I quickly became friends, and a month later, we hatched a plan to leave our families and move to neighbouring Guinea for safety. We were both exhausted by the war and desperate for a better life after years of running and hiding. But Memuna ditched the plan after she volunteered to become a ground commander in her village of Rochain, about thirty miles from Makeni. Rochain suffered persistent attacks and was overwhelmingly looted by the rebels. It was particularly targeted because most of the residents were either cattle breeders or crop farmers, so there was a lot of food in the community. As a ground commander, Memuna was the main point of contact for all decision-making and advice in her community. In a community with no health facilities, she mobilized seniors who took up the risky challenge to become traditional birth attendants and help to deliver many babies. While most of the men were hiding in the bushes, Memuna would spend much of her time either negotiating with the fighters or cooking for them to prevent them from burning down her town. As she shared with me: "I don't have the right words to describe what we experienced here, what we saw with our naked eyes, and what we did to save this community. Those stories are grim, but I'm just glad that most of us live to tell those stories."

Like Memuna, many other women in Sierra Leone have similar experiences to share. Across Sierra Leone, women like Memuna are still recognized for the role they played during the war to help their communities. Sadly though, that is not what the international world knows of women in my country and women in many other conflict areas. To some people, a survivor of a conflict only brings to mind images of an illiterate, poor, malnourished woman desperately striving to survive. While some of that may be true, largely hidden from the rest of the world is the extraordinary strength, determination, and resilience of many survivors of conflicts, especially women who also demonstrated leadership skills during those terrifying humanitarian crises. Similarly, many young survivors, male and female, played no part in the conflict, but to date, many bear the burden of defending themselves from remarks about having directly participated in the conflict wherever they go and whenever their countries are mentioned. From filling in immigration forms to community integration programs, the questions of suspicion are obvious: "Have you ever participated in a conflict?" It is also not uncommon in pubs or at social gatherings for people to ask you deeply troubling questions about the atrocities that were committed. In my case, I sometimes feel like I'm on trial and I'm being confronted with the evidence of my country's past sins! As a matter of fact, there is enough evidence that grave atrocities were committed, so there's no point in denying that. There are many encounters that force me to reflect on those dark days in my country's history.

To date, I have images of the destruction on my mind. I often think of how I ran away from my home without my family. It has been nearly twenty years now since that war was declared over; those images haven't disappeared. I see them all the time when I get reminded. But in my brain, I also have images of Memuna helping children and pregnant women. I have images of other women risking their lives to save their communities. They were ordinary people who took extraordinary measures to stitch their communities together in some of the most challenging times. I have images of smiles, fun, and hugs from loved ones after we were reunited. Those moments often make me realize how lucky I am to have survived what was described as a catastrophic conflict in which thousands of my fellow Sierra Leoneans lost their lives. To some people, we are a lost generation whose future was ruined by the war, but to many of us who experienced those difficult times, we are a generation united by a common goal, which is to rebuild our country and move on.

Don't Lose Hope: You Never Know What Tomorrow May Bring

Nareen Haj Ali and Catherine Baillie Abidi

During the three years that we have had the pleasure to get to know each other, we have shared stories of migration, resilience, and community. For the purpose of this book, we decided to record a conversation over tea at Nareen Haj Ali's home to share perspectives of how we tell stories of war and peace.

CATHERINE BAILLIE ABIDI: Nareen, as you know, the concept of the book is to explore stories of war and peace. The chapter we are doing together is intended to highlight perspectives from people who have been forced to migrate due to conflict. Thank you for agreeing to share your story. It is really important to learn from families how conflict impacts our lives and how we can build communities together. To begin, can you share a little about you and your family?

NAREEN HAJ ALI: Yes. We have four kids. We are a Kurdish family. We were living in Kobani in northern Syria, on the border with Turkey. We were living there when the war started. At that time, we suddenly discovered two of our kids had big health problems—my oldest one, and then my second one. Because our city was a little town, we needed to travel from place to place to treat them. But because of the war, we weren't free to travel. It was too dangerous to travel from city to city. The war's impact was everywhere. If you move from city to city, maybe you never come home; you are lost. That happened to many people in my city. There are around three hundred people over six years that I do not know anything about. They were travelling from our city to Aleppo to get their salary. Most of them were teachers, and many of them we do not know anything about, whether they are living.

When we discovered my two daughters had medical troubles, we travelled to Damascus to find a good doctor to treat them in a good hospital. On the way, we saw many, many dangers. There were some places that were bombed with fire everywhere. We saw many things when we went to Damascus, even in the hospital. The hospital was close to the mountain, and we saw many opposition tanks that were coming to fight.

When I took the girls to the hospital for the first time, they told us to leave the window open because, when the tanks fire, it may break the glass if they are closed. At first, the girls were hugging me, even when they were sick. I don't know how to explain that. It was too hard for me as a mom to see this happen in front of them.

CATHERINE BAILLIE ABIDI: How often did you have to travel to Damascus for their treatments?

NAREEN HAJ ALI: Because of their kidneys, we had to go every month to get their medicine and to check their blood. Many times, we couldn't go because of the situation, so we contacted the doctor. The doctor told us to stay where we are safe and to send their blood work, and he told me what medicine to give them. We went to Damascus just twice, but it was very hard. The last time we went, there was no transport back to our city, and it took seventeen days until finally we went to Turkey.

CATHERINE BAILLIE ABIDI: What was Syria like before the war?

NAREEN HAJ ALI: Syria was like any other country. It has its own traditions and its own culture. Actually, it was a very safe country before the war started. Everything was available, even education. Even we as Kurdish people, we do not have the right to take education in our language or speak in our language, but it was okay for us. Many people learned their language in secret, but the education was very good. People were studying. We had good doctors, and everything was available in Syria. It was not like how many people think of Syria now. It was actually a really nice country.

CATHERINE BAILLIE ABIDI: Tell me about your community.

NAREEN HAJ ALI: There were around three million people living in my community. In my city, all people were Kurdish. Syria had about thirty million people and around three million were Kurdish—around 10 percent. After the regime changed, the schools in my city are now teaching in Kurdish—like the Kurdish do in Iraq. But I think it is not a good education because of the war. There are no good schools. Even the teachers do not have experience teaching Kurdish.

CATHERINE BAILLIE ABIDI: What would you like the Canadian public to know about Syria now?

NAREEN HAJ ALI: I would like to tell everyone that they have to do things to bring back peace in Syria. All over the world, you find Syrian people. Syrians are very good people. They have good education. They have their own jobs.

CATHERINE BAILLIE ABIDI: What is the role of the international community in Syria? What can be done to bring back peace in Syria?

NAREEN HAJ ALI: If a country like the US wants to stop any war, they can. But they did not want to stop the war. For example, I will tell you something: when ISIS forces attacked my city, they were coming from Raqqa. ISIS took this city as the capital city for them. There is a lot of empty space in between this city and my city, so when they would come with their tanks and their stuff, everyone in the world could see they were coming. They knew they were coming. They could bomb them in the empty space, but the US, they waited—waited until they entered the city and fought with our Kurdish fighters and then they decided to help. They hunted them, ISIS, inside my city. The houses fell down, including my house. If they had fought them before they arrived, it would have been better, but they don't want that. I don't know what they were thinking.

CATHERINE BAILLIE ABIDI: Why do you think there was no intervention when violence was growing?

NAREEN HAJ ALI: I think ISIS is their industry. It is an opportunity to sell their weapons. Peace does not help them. They always want the war to continue everywhere—the big countries.

CATHERINE BAILLIE ABIDI: What is the most important part of your family's experience that you think people should know about?

NAREEN HAJ ALI: The most important thing is to take care of the kids in the war. For me it was hard—this part with my children. I think we would have been okay if their health had been okay like other kids', but I needed to keep an eye on their health. We had to travel everywhere to find the right care, and it was very hard for me as a mom. That was the hardest part, I think. The children come first.

CATHERINE BAILLIE ABIDI: Your situation was so unique with the girls because of the significance of their health situation. As a mom, what is important for other moms to think about war and peace?

NAREEN HAJ ALI: The kids come first. Every mom must take care of her kids. As a parent of two sick children, I had to make a big decision in my life to leave my job and my country. I had to make this decision because of the war in Syria. Also, I made this decision because there was not enough medical care available after the war started, so I had to leave Syria and go to Turkey. This crossing was for emergencies only. It was not easy, but after we showed a lot of medical reports, and we did a lot of paperwork, we finally left Syria. I left Syria with my husband and two sick children, but my two other children, aged three and five, stayed in Syria with our relatives. I left behind my other two children because the girls needed me more than they did. It was very difficult to leave my children in one country and go to another without knowing if I would see them again, but it was necessary to save the lives of my sick children. Saving life comes first in every situation.

CATHERINE BAILLIE ABIDI: What does peace mean to you and what does it look like?

NAREEN HAJ ALI: I think peace is when we live all together without any fighting—without any problem.

When the kids go to school, and you don't worry about them. When your kids are healthy. This is peace for me, I think. Everyone living in one country like sisters and brothers. No enemy between brothers and sisters. This is peaceful. Unfortunately, we missed that one in our country. Everyone fights each other.

CATHERINE BAILLIE ABIDI: You are a very brave woman, Nareen. It has been a pleasure to get to know you and your family. Our community has so much to learn from you. This book is about teaching and sharing stories with the hope that we can make people more aware and care more. Is there anything else that you think is important to say?

NAREEN HAJ ALI: I think we should never lose our hope. We never know what will happen tomorrow.

When we were in Turkey and the girls were in a bad situation, I never lost my hope and was always thinking, *tomorrow will be better. Tomorrow will be better.* I never stopped. I tried many times to contact the US and many organizations to get our kids help. Finally, we got the chance to come to Canada, and in Canada, they had very good treatment and they are healthy and are very happy.

My Story

Viyan Ali

Let me start by telling you who I am and what made me this way. I may sound like every other teenager, but I have a story to tell. Where I come from, everyone has a different story that makes them resilient.

As a little kid I never knew what war, peace, or being scared meant. The only thing I was scared of was the monster that could come out of my closet at nighttime, which is what every kid is scared of. But I did always wonder what war was and why it happens. In 2011, the war first started in Syria, and at the time it was all over the TV but I didn't believe it. You know when your parents say that a lot of things on TV are not real? At that time, I thought the war was not real and it was like a TV show or maybe that was what I wanted to believe. Kids my age, families, and others were getting killed. By the time I realized that it was real, and it was happening, people started demonstrations for their freedom and peace. I remember going out to participate in one of the demonstrations for the first time, and it felt weird. I felt like there were butterflies in my stomach. I was a little afraid of what was going to happen because of what I saw on the TV. But it was okay.

After a few years, in 2013, I had to go to the capital of Syria, Damascus, for medical reasons. In the place I lived at that time, there was nothing dangerous other than not having enough water and electricity. But on the way to the capital, there were a lot of barriers, and each barrier belonged to a different military unit. At each barrier, we would wait around ten to thirty minutes so the guards could check everyone's IDs. When I arrived in the capital, the place I never dreamt to go to, the first thing I saw was fires and buildings that were torn to pieces. When we arrived at the safe place, I heard that we were being sent to the other side, which they call the enemy side, *but were they the enemies?*

After a few weeks, I went back to my town, my town that I call the safe place. It was safe but it was hard to live in. Even though there was a war, people still loved my town because it was where family and loved ones were. After a few months, I had to go to Damascus again, but this time, when going there, there was a sniper who was shooting every bus that went by. As soon as we passed that place, the driver drove really fast. I heard a little something but I didn't think it could be it. After a while, the driver slowed down and asked if everyone was okay. We were lucky the bullets hit the back of the bus and no one was sitting there. The sniper hit one of the windows on a bus before us, and someone hurt themselves with the window glass.

After a few weeks, we went back to our town. Then we headed to Turkey, but this time, we had to leave two family members behind, thinking that we'll only be gone for two to three days, but we stayed for more than one month. My dad went back to our town to bring my other two siblings, but no one knew that he would end up bringing the whole town with him. After a few weeks, my dad was still in Syria, and we heard that ISIS was trying to get into our town. Everyone was trying to get out of the town as soon as possible. I remember how scared I was there. All kinds of things were going through my mind, like, *are they going to be okay, is everyone going to be safe, is Turkey going to let people come into the city or would they just watch?* After a day, people started coming to Turkey. A lot of people went to refugee camps. It was the longest week of my life. Time stood still. The news was on the TV all the time.

After a few months, a lot of things were back to normal, but not exactly. Most places were destroyed. Some people went back. Others just stayed because they did not have anything to go back to. Everything they had was destroyed. My family did not go back like the others. Now we were living in Turkey. I did not go to school for the first few months in Turkey. I eventually went to an Arabic school.

I stopped dreaming because I didn't see the dreams ever coming to reality. I suppose I could tell you what the dreams that I stopped dreaming of were. Well, to be honest, I always wanted to continue my education and become a journalist. But how could I now go to university and become what I wanted to be? When this happened to Syria, I didn't think I would be able to accomplish my dreams. I threw them away as if they were a piece of old paper that had been shredded to pieces. But I never gave up hope that Syria could become like before—full of peace. For me, life kept going. It was okay. I got used to it.

After a few years, in 2016, we got a call asking if we would like to go to Canada. We were surprised and, of course, we said yes. After a few months of paperwork, it was finally the day of our plane ride to Canada. When I was on the plane, I didn't believe I was going to Canada, and on the way, I was thinking a lot. Was I finally going somewhere peaceful? Was I going to start a new and happy chapter of my life? When I arrived, I didn't know English, but I could tell that everyone was so welcoming and happy. It was the most peaceful feeling I had in years.

Now it has been years since I came to Canada. Currently, I'm going to start grade 11. Also, pretty soon I'm going to get my citizenship. It is amazing how years can fly by, and you can't feel it. All of this leads me to what I want to study, and I can't wait to study journalism. Do I miss Syria? Well, of course, I do, but now I'm used to being here, and I don't think I could leave it, but Syria will always be a part of me. Let's not forget Canada is my home too. I'm really thankful for Canada, and I don't know if it will ever be enough how many times I thank Canada. In the end, I feel peace because of it. My story has come to an end but my journey, well, it's only beginning.

No Red Poppies for Colombia

Marianela Fuertes

Where you are born is a random fact. By luck some are born in peaceful, prosperous, stable, and civilized democracies. Others are born in places devastated by violence. And that random fact defines all in your life, even your right to transit and to move as you please in this world. My family and I were not lucky. We were born in a country that did not even have a decade of peace. How should I talk about it to help create understanding, especially without eliciting pity? What is the relevance of my story when we live with an overwhelming number of stories about refugees who are running for their lives? I do not have an answer, but I hope my story can contribute in some way to put a face to this ocean of displacement, suffering, and despair. Also, I would like to give an idea of the important role Canada has been playing around the world. I think I can accomplish this by highlighting the contrast between being born and growing up in a country experiencing a long and awful internal war and living in a nation facing other kinds of armed conflicts, especially conflicts between formal armies in an international confrontation. Also, I want to distinguish the situation of a refugee from that of an immigrant. Refugees do not have an option. They have to leave their countries to protect their lives.

I was born and grew up in Colombia, a South American country where the internal armed conflict does not have a precise start date that anyone can agree on. One can trace the violence that characterizes Colombia's history back to the Spanish conquest and their search for El Dorado. Then the leaders and members of the independence movements fought among themselves over the conquest's benefits and wealth. Those movements were the origin of the political parties who built their identities on trying to obliterate the opposition. At first, the fighting occurred between the parties and then, during the Cold War, those traditional parties joined forces to fight anyone who dissented or clamoured for a strong state capable of providing justice and security for all its citizens. In consequence, it is possible to find armed confrontation at each stage of Colombian history.

The armed conflict in Colombia over the past fifty years is the result of a combination of political, economic, and social factors. The weakness of the state, which makes it unable to provide security and uphold the rule of law, is self-evident. The state's presence is very precarious, especially in rural areas far from the centre of the country where the big cities are located. A large portion of the country has been left under the control of criminal groups, which sometimes even receive the support of the army and the police. Any calls to overcome inequality or to point out the lack of basic services and the weakness or non-existence of the rule of law have been framed by the state as radical left-wing ideas. As such, in Colombia, principles that are fundamental to democracy have been branded by the state as dangerous to the nation—akin to guerrilla ideologies. That dynamic has illegitimatized efforts aiming to create the basic foundations of civil and democratic society. On the contrary, the political conflict has promoted violence as a viable political tactic for the government and for the opposition. The conflict has bred multiple guerrilla groups—inspired by communist ideology—including the oldest guerrilla group in Latin America: the FARC (Revolutionary Armed Forces of Colombia). The FARC has been fighting against the government, who are mainly landlords, powerful families, and those who have the economic power. In 2018, the government and the FARC signed a peace agreement, but the peace is in a very precarious state because the new president came from the party that does not support the agreement. The FARC's right-wing counterparts are the paramilitary groups. These paramilitaries are often financed by ranchers, landowners, and drug traffickers, and they are frequently associated with the national army forces. These groups make up the landscape of the war in Colombia. The internal armed conflict, in contrast with an international war, is like a war between members of the same family. Hate and resentment become ingrained and are passed down from generation to generation. Nobody wins in that endless tragedy.

Within this context, my story as a human rights lawyer who had to leave her country represents the situation of a great number of professionals who believe in justice and have worked in human rights. Many of these workers are not as fortunate as my husband and me, and are not able to escape their persecutors. My husband and I were working in the justice system. I was a constitutional and human rights lawyer, and he was a public prosecutor for crimes against humanity and serious crimes against human rights. Our entire careers were dedicated to defending human rights and pursuing the supremacy of the rule of law. We were first-hand witnesses to the consequences of the violence, perfidy, and evil of the armed conflict, and we always pursued peace, justice, and the rule of law. We worked to make our country a civilized and democratic place to live in and raise our son. We did not think that we would be forced to leave. Perhaps we were naive or reckless for dedicating our lives to defending human rights in a country where the rule of law only exists as a farce to hide abuse and corruption, but we were not the only ones.

We did not want to even think of leaving the country despite knowing the problems, risks, and violence that lie in wait. We were part of a process that was constructing a new deal for Colombia: a new constitution, new institutions, and new tools for democracy. We believed that we had an opportunity to see substantial changes in Colombia. This resolve gave us the courage to face dangerous situations, such as being detained by a guerrilla group on the road and then being caught in the crossfire between them and the army. Neither the guerrillas nor the soldiers cared about all the defenceless civilians, as Colombian history has shown repeatedly. My husband's name was at the top of the list that the paramilitaries published, threatening the prosecutors who investigated them for their massacres. The head of the United Self-Defence Forces of Colombia, Carlos Castaño Gil, who was responsible for hundreds of murders and publicly recognized as a drug trafficker, called me to say that the published list of public prosecutors—topped by my husband—was authentic, and he wanted to make it clear that he knew us.

Danger—being the targets of the armed groups—was a constant condition in our lives and jobs, but also in the lives of all people who were trying to live without violence. A large number of brave and dedicated human rights activists, judges, social justice leaders, union leaders, and teachers have been killed in this amorphous and evil war. We never doubted that it was our duty to contribute to creating a democracy where life and freedom were respected. We were not waiting to jump on a plane at the first opportunity we had to leave. On the contrary, it is important to emphasize that when the threats got more severe and the military intelligence service—known for serious violations of human rights—began taking pictures of our three-year-old boy, and the prosecutor's office where my husband worked decided to remove his security measures, we entered a spiral of helplessness: living long days without any idea about our future, watching over our shoulders, looking for threats, feeling that people were growing distant. Nowhere felt safe. We felt like we were living on borrowed time.

It is with great respect for the experiences of other survivors and victims of armed conflicts that I humbly share my story, in hopes of promoting learning and understanding. Also, I feel guilty in some way when I think about all the people I knew who were killed. In the sixth month of my pregnancy, two human rights workers, Elsa Alvarado and Mario Calderon, were killed in their apartment. The killers—who were members of the paramilitary forces associated with the government army—broke into their home and killed them in front of their little boy's crib. That boy is now twenty-two years old. I walked in a peace march in honour of them with a flower on my belly, crying for them and terrified for my future. We are lucky that we could escape the death threats and fly with our little boy to this generous land. How many people cannot do that? I am lucky, but still cry for them.

Thanks to a couple of good friends who knew about our situation and were working in an international human rights office, we received the aid that helped save our lives. In two weeks, we packed up our lives and, after a long flight, landed in a place where we did not know anyone or anything. I remember, four months after arriving in Canada, I started to see that people were wearing a red flower on their coat lapel. I did not know why. It was at the English as a Second Language class where I learned the meaning. We read the poem "In Flanders Fields." Also, the news, shows, and movies were discussing and showing stories about the Second World War. All of them were talking about how humanity was protected from the Nazi horror and how good triumphed over evil, and how Canada was part of that. Everywhere, you could find symbols of pride, honour, and heroism. The contrast was huge. Thinking about the fifty years of war in my country, I could not find any honour or pride, and there was certainly no sign of triumph of good over evil. Destruction, violence, torture, massacres, kidnappings, bombings, orphanhood, horror, fear, and a profound sense of helplessness were the scenes my physical, mental, and spiritual memory relived and will continue to relive forever.

We learned to love this country that opened its door to us. We have met amazing, kind, and generous people, and our son has had the opportunity to grow and become a genuine, bright, faithful, trustworthy young man committed to making this world a better place. We were welcomed in this generous land that saved our lives. Now I keep hoping to eventually feel like I belong.

Chapter 4

African Nova Scotian Communities

Introduction

Susan M. Brigham

A country's dominant narratives are sustained through a combination of public and private events and teachings, including special holidays, traditions, symbols, school curricula, and popular culture. These narratives often come to represent pride, honour, and patriotism for many, yet the making of these narratives requires a certain amount of wilful forgetfulness, mythmaking, and denial by the dominant group in power of non-dominant perspectives, realities, and historical and present-day facts. In Canada, the hegemony of colonialism, Eurocentricity, white supremacy, patriarchy, and elitism combine to reduce complicated realities to simplified stories. For example, stories of early settlement of Canada's frontiers shine a spotlight on the brave industrious European colonial pioneers, while in the shadows, colonial powers meted out violence on enslaved Black women, men, and children labouring to survive and on Indigenous communities experiencing cultural genocide. Similarly, stories of Canada's efforts in the world wars highlight heroic white men on the front lines, while racialized minorities and women become mere footnotes. Yet, they were also on the battlefields working in field hospitals, on ambulance trains, and in construction battalions, or back home running farms and businesses and caring for children and elders in homes and institutions. Emma Battell Lowman and Adam J. Barker draw attention to the dominant story of Canada as a peacekeeping nation, which they refer to as a peacemaker myth. They write,

> *The peacemaker myth is tightly entangled with the perception of Canada as a multicultural mosaic. It is a story of a Canada that, while once troubled by racial strife, has achieved enlightenment, and now welcomes all people as equals, with the same rights and responsibilities, the same respect and dignity, regardless of where they may come from or how and why they have come to the lands we all now share. And it underpins the idea of Canada as an international leader. We are the little country that could, that fought on the "right" side of both World Wars, that helped found the United Nations, that is a peacekeeping nation in international conflicts, that is a paragon of justice, free of corruption, ranked among the best places to live and the envy of many other nations, and with absolutely "no history of colonialism," in the words of [former Prime Minister] Stephen Harper (Battell Lowman and Barker 2015, 45).*

Such national narratives idealize a Canada that allows some citizens to feel at home and others to feel like they do not belong. Anthony Stewart describes this feeling of not belonging as being a visitor—not an invited guest but someone, like a tourist, who is to be tolerated until they leave. The visitors are usually those who do not trace their lineage to Western Europe and "do not conventionally 'look' Canadian.... White Canadians in other words" (Stewart 2014, 18–19). This exclusion "combined with discriminatory behaviours in classrooms, biased institutional policies, as well as stereotypes and negative portrayals of certain groups in the media reinforce and sustain systems of domination" (Brigham 2013, 120).

Even while dominant stories and myths persist, not everyone accepts them unquestioningly, especially as critical historians and family and community members contribute diverse counter-stories of, for example, African-descendant and Indigenous Peoples' resistance, activism, and leadership. A critical perspective that puts Black people and their historical and cultural experiences at the centre of analysis is Africentricity.[1] Africentricity involves a decolonization process of rediscovering and recovering one's history, culture, language, and identity

(Chilisa 2012). The goal is to expose, resist, and challenge European-centredness and oppressive racist beliefs of African inferiority and to understand how these beliefs have been assimilated into society and into the lives of people of African descent, and how this, for some, results in self-hatred and internalized oppression (Asante 2003). Achieving this goal requires what is represented by the Sankofa bird, an Asante Adinkra symbol depicting a bird moving forward with her head turned backward, holding an egg in her mouth: a reminder that the knowledge of the past cannot be forgotten and that, in order to move ahead, we need to retrieve the wisdom of the past to help future generations. The Sankofa bird is symbolic of Africentricity.

In this chapter, two authors take an Africentric perspective to examine the involvement of people of African descent in peace and war (particularly in the period of the First World War). Claudine Bonner and Sylvia Parris-Drummond centre their pieces on the experiences of Black people in the Canadian military. They highlight Black people's active participation in building and defending a country that has not always welcomed them or included them in the dominant narrative. Bonner and Parris-Drummond both challenge the limited military history of Black Canadians, reminding us that while many stories exist, they are pushed out of the frame of the nation's self-image. Their contributions emerge through an understanding of what Blackness means in Canada, not only historically in times of war, but also in contemporary times. They serve to remind Canadians to acknowledge what Black people have done for the country and what the country has done to Black people.

Bonner argues that the makeup of the Canadian military requires a discussion of the diasporic movement of people of African descent throughout the Americas. She shows how relations within the British Empire shaped their experiences of military service. This broader perspective sets the context for Parris-Drummond's contribution in which she reflects on her family story focusing on her father, Joseph A. Parris, who signed up to fight in the First World War.

Parris-Drummond blends facts and imaginings to create a space to talk about the impact of war beyond the battlefields and the ways in which her father's experiences in the No. 2 Construction Battalion—also known as the Black Battalion—affected the family and community over generations. Both pieces reinforce the critical Africentric aim, which is to bring to the centre of analysis the multiplicity of histories and narratives of African-descendant people as a way to help disrupt the dominant narrative, not only of war and peace, but also of life in general. As the Nigerian proverb goes, "Until the lions have their own historians, the history of the hunt will always glorify the hunter."

NOTES

1 Susan M. Brigham uses *Africentricity*, not *Afrocentricity*. While both are often used interchangeably, Brigham uses *Africentricity* for two reasons: First, *Afri* is from *African*. Second, it follows how the spelling evolved in Canada generally and in Nova Scotia specifically. For example, the only Black-focused school in Canada opened in Toronto in 2009, and it is called the Africentric School. In the Faculty of Education at Mount Saint Vincent University, Brigham coordinated and taught in master of education cohorts designated for students of African descent, which were called the Africentric cohorts; the courses included the term *Africentric*. She has also co-edited a book, among the first from Nova Scotia on the topic, called *Theorizing Africentricity in Action: Who We Are Is What We See* (Bernard and Brigham 2012). She has further published on the topic using the spelling *Africentricity* (e.g., Brigham 2022). Also see Javed (2008) for a discussion of the use of *Afro* versus *Afri*.

Canadian Military History and the Black Atlantic

Claudine Bonner

My father left Jamaica at the age of sixteen to join the Royal Air Force in the final years of the Second World War. As a result, I grew up with a particular set of understandings about the experiences of Black soldiers in Britain and elsewhere during wartime. I have always been interested in the ways the British Empire related to demonstrations of patriotism and citizenship. With a "proudly British" dad who also held Jamaican and American passports, I knew questions of citizenship and identity were never easily answered and that, for some, the realities of colonialism and imperialism could shape fluid identities, contingent on context. Growing up, many of my friends had very similar experiences, some having been born in the United Kingdom or in Canada as a result of their fathers' military time in either place.

As a child, however, I had no understanding of the ways that the stories of my friends, and so many of my own small personal family tales, were—and still are—connected to a greater narrative. My father's story highlights the ways in which young men from throughout the British Empire had previously joined, and continue to join, waves of movement from and within the Caribbean and the broader African diaspora. Throughout the empire, people of African descent have served in colonial and other military conflicts for hundreds of years. Even within the context of Canadian military history, people of

African descent, whilst often forgotten in the telling, have participated in uniform, dating back to the American Revolution (Ruck 1986).

Children educated in the Canadian school system have not always had access to the historical presence of people of African descent in Canada. While there have been notable efforts to uncover the narratives of African Canadians, some would say such research is still only in its beginning stages. Calls continue for more research and scholarship expanding the knowledge of Canada's place in the geography of the Black Atlantic, as well as the role of African Canadians in the history of this nation. In truth, as Peter James Hudson and Aaron Kamugisha argue:

> *For while Canada is often reduced to a static, one-dimensional geography (as the last stop on the Underground Railroad, as the promised land under the North Star), the country has in fact been both a staging ground and refuge for successive generations of Black migrants, exiles, refugees, and visitors, from the seventeenth century to the present, and from the West Indies to East Africa (2014, 3).*

In response, I examine Black Canadian military history using an African diasporic lens and argue that the makeup of the Canadian military can be seen as a case for discussion of the diasporic movement of people of African descent throughout the Americas. By providing two Nova Scotian examples, I highlight the continued presence of people of African descent and their active participation in building, defending, and championing a country that has not always been welcoming to them.

The movement of people within this region can be examined by looking at four waves, beginning with the Atlantic slave trade, which resulted in the mass movement and dispersal of millions of Africans into the Caribbean and the Americas. Slaves were sold and exchanged within and between geographic regions until prevented by legislation, resulting in a reshaping of the physical and cultural landscapes of the places in which they settled. Places such as Barbados and Jamaica were markets for products from the Carolinas, and this world of trade included the exchange of bodies. The displacement wrought by the Atlantic slave trade was followed by a second wave, a massive movement of people from the British West Indies and into the Americas at the turn of the twentieth century. Extreme changes in industry and urbanization worked to fuel the movement of people worldwide. Following this period, there was little movement until a third wave from 1930 to the 1960s, when countries like the US and Canada relaxed restrictions on immigration for members of previously undesired races, and there was a massive influx of Caribbean migrants. Most research looking at the migration of African Caribbean people into Canada focuses on the third wave of migration, and especially the major influx of Caribbean people into the major centres in Canada in the 1960s. The fourth wave is the contemporary movement of people of African descent into the Americas and beyond.

The examination of movements within these multiple trajectories typifies recent scholarship in New World African diaspora studies. These studies explore the constant movement of Black people and the complex networks within which they exchanged ideas, goods, and cultural capital (Gilroy 1993). As historian Afua Cooper (2009) has pointed out, diaspora communities and experiences are created due to migrations, forced or otherwise. While much of the literature focuses solely on the Atlantic slave trade and its impact, scholars now agree on the importance of acknowledging the notion of diaspora as being an "organic process involving movement from an ancestral land, settlement in new lands, and...[sometimes] renewed settlement and movement elsewhere" (Palmer 1998, 22). So, we can speak of individuals such as Marie-Joseph Angélique, a Black Portuguese slave woman in New France, as embodying double or triple diasporic identities resulting from their origins and the migratory experiences of enslavement (Cooper 2007).

Diasporic movements led to the arrival in Canada of Black Refugees from the War of 1812. During that war, British Admiral

Alexander Cochrane's proclamation of 1814 offered freedom to any enslaved person willing to fight on the side of the British and to those who could escape enslavement and make their way behind British lines. This offer included resettlement in the British colonies, and as a result, by the end of the conflict, over two thousand formerly enslaved persons had resettled in Nova Scotia (Whitfield 2006). Black men fought in non-segregated units such as the 104th Regiment and the Glengarry Light Infantry during the War of 1812, and they worked to defend the government during the Upper Canada Rebellion from 1837 to 1839 (Ruck 1986). William Hall, perhaps the best-known person of African descent in Canadian military history, was born in Nova Scotia's Annapolis Valley in 1827, the child of refugees from the War of 1812. In 1852, Hall enlisted in the Royal Navy in Liverpool, England, after having served in the American merchant navy. He would go on to have a distinguished naval career, serving first in the Crimean War and later in India on HMS *Shannon*. As a result of his service, he was awarded the Victoria Cross, the British Empire's highest honour for bravery; the first person of African descent, the first Nova Scotian, and in fact, the first Canadian sailor to receive this honour (Blakeley 1957; Pachai 2003).

Despite the presence of Black men like Hall in military roles dating from the American Revolution and well into the late nineteenth century, Black men seeking to enlist at the outbreak of the First World War were routinely turned away from recruiting stations across the country, even though there was no official legislation denying their enlistment. According to Walker, this was in keeping with the general sentiments surrounding the concept of *race* during this period (Walker 1989). For nearly two years, Canadian Blacks and other visible minorities petitioned the government, seeking to enlist in the armed forces as part of their national duty. In addition to duty, many also saw enlisting as a way for them and their communities to be recognized as people in contexts where they continued to be treated as second-class citizens (Walker 1989). Among this group were many recently arrived Caribbean migrants who settled in Whitney Pier in Cape Breton. Several of these men had made their way to Whitney Pier seeking opportunities for employment in the steel industry. The Dominion Iron and Steel Company drew them to the community and many of the men would be employed by this company until their retirement.

Henry Isaac Phills, the first person of African descent to receive the Order of Canada, was part of this migratory movement within the Americas. Born in St. Vincent in 1896, Phills had come to Canada in 1916 in search of work opportunities. In 1917, as Canada struggled to meet its commitments to the war effort, the Borden government passed the 1917 Military Service Act, a law introducing conscription. As a result, many were forced to enlist. Phills was conscripted, and he served in the 1st Depot Battalion, NS Regiment, during the war. Despite having opened up access to racialized groups as a result of conscription, the Canadian military still struggled with issues of integration. According to Calvin W. Ruck, Phills was one of about sixty Black men in his unit. When they arrived in England, there had been talk of assigning them to a segregated unit or to the No. 2 Construction Battalion, the battalion in the Canadian Expeditionary Force (CEF) designated for Black soldiers. They were instead used as reinforcements for the 85th Battalion, perhaps out of necessity (Ruck 1986).

The makeup of the No. 2 Construction Battalion is perhaps most indicative of the diasporic movement of people of African descent shaping Canadian military history. In response to the initial refusal to admit Black men to the CEF, Black Canadians had openly challenged the government (Winks 1971). Extensive pressure was placed on both the military and on the country's government by members of the clergy, educators, and community leaders. A long series of letters and petitions survive, bearing witness to the determination of African Canadians to demonstrate their loyalty to Canada and to the Crown. The No. 2 Construction Battalion received authorization on July 5, 1916, and recruited men from across the nation. At their peak strength, the battalion was made up of 605 men of all ranks from across Canada, the Caribbean, and the US, with the sole Black officer being their captain and chaplain, Reverend William A. White (Ruck 1986). The Canada to which they returned was quite different from the one they had left. With the men having gone off to war, communities had called upon women and workers of colour, including more Caribbean migrants, to take on their jobs in the factories, in the mines, and elsewhere. Black employees gained access to spaces of employment that had previously been closed to them (Mathieu 2010).

Scholarship on the military history of Black Canadians has been limited, especially in terms of explorations by specialized military historians. Yet, many stories of the experiences of Blacks in the Canadian military exist. If we acknowledge them, we can reframe the ways we might examine Canada's military history. Viewing the people who served in the military through the lens of the Black Atlantic, taking it as a site of constant multidirectional movement between Africa, Europe, North America, and the Caribbean highlights the ways in which those who ended up serving in the various units came to do so as a result of long-standing relations within the British Empire.

My Voice and My Daddy's Story: His Time in the No. 2 Construction Battalion

Sylvia Parris-Drummond

In my African Nova Scotian heritage, I acknowledge our ancestors on whose shoulders we are perched and thank them for their resilience over generations and throughout our challenging history. It is because of them we survive, and we thrive. I acknowledge and thank Calvin W. Ruck for his work documenting the history of the Black Battalion. His spirit permeates all stories and memories of the battalion. I thank him for his vision, determination, and persistence. What I want to share in this story includes a quest for freedom and justice that is rooted deeply in family and community pride and intergenerational connectedness.

One of the pictures often used to depict the No. 2 Construction Battalion features Joseph Alexander Parris, my father. Seeing it always evokes many emotions for me, including pride, sadness, curiosity, and disappointment. Certainly, he is shown as a strapping figure in a smart uniform. He looks self-assured, a young man with purpose and resolve. I wonder what promises of adventure he had been told, or perhaps had told himself, that enticed him to join the battalion. I wish I knew more about his personal journey, about the story of the battalion and its contributions to the freedom that resulted from the First World War.

On July 25, 1916, my father, at the age of seventeen (he would not be eighteen for another nine months) enlisted in the No. 2 Construction Battalion, known as the Black Battalion. He would have made the journey from Sand Point to New Glasgow to join this labour battalion that recruited African Canadians across the country.

Imagine a seventeen-year-old boy and his brother talking with animation and verve about the war while doing their chores, perhaps working a field crop or tending farm animals. They are talking about enlisting and wanting, indeed needing, to fight for their country. Maybe they later speak with their father (my grandfather) who tries to explain to them how their race would affect their dreams. Maybe their mother (my grandmother, the midwife who delivers all the babies in the area) gets involved in the conversation and tries desperately to discourage them, not wanting to lose her sons to war.

Maybe their mother's plea is behind the reason for why the two young men enlist separately, weeks apart, in two separate locations. Perhaps it was in their blood, as the saying goes, this desire to support a cause for freedom. My grandfather, Charles L. Parris, was either of Black Loyalist or Black Refugee lineage; most likely, Black Loyalist. Both groups supported the British and came to Nova Scotia seeking to build a life for themselves and their families. The drive to fight was rooted in survival.

Bruce MacDonald wrote about my father, whom he refers to as *Joe*, in his blog, *First World War Veterans of Guysborough County*: "Like many young men of his generation, Joe was excited at the prospect of serving overseas after the outbreak of the war in Europe. His African Nova Scotian heritage, however, presented an obstacle as the majority of infantries refused to accept 'black' recruits" (2004). This was the case even though policy said otherwise.

The creation of the No. 2 Construction Battalion is an example of the Black community's agency and resilience. The community continually agitated for inclusion in the fight for freedom. It used the tools that are still in play today, such as leadership in the church and community organizing. For example, Reverend William A. White, who became the chaplain of the battalion, advocated for Black Nova Scotian men to be involved in the war. Truro became a recruiting hub because of its Black population.

The role of a construction unit was a dangerous one. It supported the front lines, building roads and bridges, defusing land mines so advancing troops could move forward, and evacuating the wounded. The men of the No. 2 Construction Battalion, who were not provided with weapons, put themselves in harm's way by choice for a country that devalued them because of their race. How can we not be in awe of such a resilient and purpose-focused community? How can I not be in awe and puff with pride at the man I call Daddy?

I am filled with questions that I would have loved to have asked Daddy, such as, "What did it feel like to sail overseas? Did you see your brother, my uncle Bill, after departing the ship? Did you miss your parents?" I was not able to ask these and many other questions for a number of reasons. The most significant reason was that this important part of Canada's history was never taught to me in public school. We did not have easy access to the full story of the Black Battalion's role in the First World War. I think now of the conversations that I could have initiated with my father had I had more knowledge. "Daddy, today I learned in school about the No. 2 Construction Battalion. The teacher said we should ask our families about it." Imagine what sharing that might have evoked. The other reason I never got to ask Daddy my questions is because he went home to glory on April 19, 1972, at the age of seventy-three when I was only fifteen. Prior to his passing, he was very ill and not able to communicate verbally for about two years.

Before either of us were the age of majority and able to vote, both Daddy and I were making momentous choices. He went to war where he would continually fight for his dignity while engaging in physical battles. I fought for family unity as I played the role of mother–sister to my baby sister who was fourteen years old when our mother died. I learned much about family pride and community pride from my father, and much about commitment and responsibility from both of my parents.

Figure 1. Five men from the Black Battalion, with Joseph Alexander Parris in the centre.
(THE BLACK CULTURAL CENTRE FOR NOVA SCOTIA, CHERRY BROOK)

My career and vocation have been entwined in education. Today in my role as chief executive officer for the Delmore "Buddy" Daye Learning Institute, which promotes excellence in Africentric education, one of my key responsibilities is to support the development of educational resource materials for schools and the broader community. These resources enable us to learn about Nova Scotia's full history by ensuring we know about African Nova Scotian history and the contributions of African Nova Scotians. I take the opportunity in front of me seriously as a mother and grandmother, and in my various kinship roles as an auntie and a senior in our community, to draw from our distant and immediate histories to embed pride in community.

Chapter 5

Military Histories Across Communities

Introduction

Tracy Moniz

This chapter sets diverse military histories side by side—the dominant narrative that connects war and military conflict to patriotism and historical remembrance alongside the lesser-known stories of Canadians who had to fight for a place on the front lines. It brings to life what historian Robert Teigrob describes as "the legacy of the national wartime experience"—that is, "a blend of celebration (particularly where deeds of heroism can be mustered as evidence) and silence (particularly where experiences and actions do not ennoble the nation's image)" (2016, 4). With respect to the latter, such counternarratives challenge the dominant military history and raise questions about the ideals of nationalism, citizenship, freedom, and justice deeply entrenched in Canada's war history.

Teigrob suggests that Canadians may be more militaristic than is typically perceived and perhaps even rival Americans, meaning that, as a society, we share "a romanticized view of soldiers, a tendency to see military power as the truest sense of national greatness, and outsized expectations regarding the efficacy of force" (Bacevich quoted in Teigrob 2016, 5). The history of Canada at war is dominated by facts and stories about military conflict that span centuries and continents. It is a story about heroic soldiers and honoured veterans, patriotism and sacrifice, battlefields and bombings, gratitude and remembrance. It is a story about military victory and the people and places that have come to symbolize it. The result for Canadians may be "deference to an epic version of its military past" (Teigrob 2016, 7).

Halifax has played a central role in Canada's war story, notably in both world wars where the city was a major strategic port. It was the chief port of North America for the first two years of the Second World War, before the US joined the war in 1941. The impact of its wartime history is etched into public memory and city landscapes. In fact, Haligonians are reminded of the city's military history every day at noon when, in tribute to it, a cannon is fired on Citadel Hill.

This history is documented and shared by the Army Museum Halifax Citadel, a private non-profit institution that promotes Atlantic Canada's military heritage, focusing on Nova Scotia in particular. In this chapter, Ken Hynes, the chief curator of the Army Museum, writes about Halifax's rich military history. His essay, "Soul of a Nation in the Heart of Halifax," highlights the role of the Army Museum in commemorating Nova Scotian veterans and the province's legacy of war and conflict, with an emphasis on the human cost of war in the region. Hynes reflects on how this legacy continues to shape our nation today. He takes readers to some of the markers of the human cost of war that the Army Museum has placed throughout the city, such as The Last Steps Memorial Arch on the waterfront that indicates the spot where 350,000 Canadians embarked for the First World War. Spaces like these prompt passersby to think about those who departed for war overseas, some never to return.

The dominant military history of war persists, in part, because of "the dearth of counter-narratives to the tales of military glory that have long populated English-Canadian books, popular culture, and media" (Teigrob 2016, 6). Such counter-narratives are emerging to offer a look behind the "military glory" to tell a broader and more inclusive history of Canada at war, one that captures the inequities of military recruitment, enlistment, and service, and the experiences of diverse groups in wartime (Teigrob 2016, 6). These groups include volunteers who tried to join the military but were rejected for various reasons (Clarke 2015), individuals who joined the military under the legal age of enlistment (Black and Boileau 2013), soldiers who experienced injustice because of race or ethnicity (Fowler 2016; Winegard 2019), and foreign workers exploited for their military labour (Black 2019a; Black 2019b). As an example of the latter, Dan Black's book on the Chinese Labour Corps tells the story of a group of Chinese labourers recruited to support Britain during the First World War. They worked "behind the lines to keep the war machine in motion—digging trenches, stacking ammunition, hauling supplies, repairing military vehicles and the grisly job of cleaning up the battlefields" (Black 2019a; Black 2019b). Their labour released other men for front-line duty. About eighty-one thousand members of the Chinese Labour Corps travelled secretly by train across Canada to Halifax where they sailed for France (Black 2019a). How many Canadians know this piece of Canada's war story?

This chapter adds two counter-narratives to the historiography of Canada at war, each about a community that would presumably not show interest in fighting a war for Britain or even Canada, given the complexities of their respective histories and the brutalities of colonial history. Yet, members of Indigenous and Acadian communities in Nova Scotia voluntarily enlisted, carving a place for themselves in times of war despite biases and exclusionary practices and policy.

In "We Were There: Remembering Nova Scotia's Mi'kmaw War Veterans," Mi'kmaw historian Don Julien tells of the Mi'kmaw veterans who enlisted in Nova Scotia to serve in the First World War. In this Q&A with Jenna Stewart, he shares facts and anecdotes from his archival research about the ninety Indigenous people from Nova Scotia that his work has traced—from details of their names and regimental numbers to stories of their haphazard and, at times, discouraged enlistment; their sacrifices at war; and their readjustment to life postwar for those who returned to their communities in Nova Scotia. Julien also engages with the question of what it meant to be an Indigenous person overseas in contexts of war and peacekeeping. Along the way, his language shifts—from *Indian* and *First Nation* to *Indigenous* and, specifically *Mi'kmaw* veteran—reminiscent of the shifting use of language over time. This contribution offers a local slice of a larger Canadian narrative about Indigenous people in the First World War who, due to "social biases and public opinion" were discouraged from enlisting and, in fact, were not viewed as a source of recruits for military service at all (Winegard 2019, 12–13). Recruitment for war eventually changed when the need for personnel became critical, and Britain then called on the military to include Indigenous people. Historian Timothy Winegard calls the increased participation of Indigenous people in the First World War "the potential pivotal catalyst to accelerate the attainment of equal rights" because they, like all who went to war, sacrificed, shed blood, and died (2019, 13). Julien's contribution to this collection reminds Canadians of the legacy of Nova Scotia's Indigenous people at war—that they were, in fact, there on the battlefields.

Historian Gregory Kennedy also adds to the historiography of the First World War by delving into the story of another group that had to fight for a place in Canada's war—the Acadians in the Baie Sainte-Marie region of Nova Scotia. Kennedy traces the turbulent history of this group, who comprised the first Europeans to settle in the province in the 1600s, in what was then the French territory of Acadie (Nova Scotia Archives 2020). The Acadians who later lobbied to fight in the First World War were the descendants of those who had eventually returned to Atlantic Canada after Britain's forced deportation of this French population from the province between 1755 and 1763. In the process of this expulsion, their homes, farms, and other possessions were seized and destroyed, and the Acadians were left to disperse to other areas of North America as well as to the Caribbean and to Europe (Nova Scotia Archives 2020). This event stands as a "defining moment in the history of the Acadian French in Atlantic Canada" and, as such, it would stand to reason that the descendants of those evicted would bear the weight of that history and be less inclined to enlist and fight a war for Canada or Britain (Nova Scotia Archives 2020). But, as Kennedy explains, despite their difficult history and presence as a linguistic minority, at the time of the First World War, many Acadians viewed military service as an opportunity for the nation to recognize their contributions. After successfully lobbying the Canadian government, an Acadian national battalion—the 165th Battalion—was created in 1915. Drawing on a range of archival materials including military records and census reports, Kennedy details the history of this Acadian unit, focusing on the contingent of eighty-six recruits from Baie Sainte-Marie and, in particular, four brothers from the Saulnier family who enlisted.

These military histories of Nova Scotia's Indigenous and Acadian communities bring to the forefront issues of citizenship. Who is a citizen? Who belongs? Who doesn't? How do notions of citizenship intersect with race, ethnicity, sex, and gender? With military service? Amid a national push for Canadians to enlist for war, neither group—the Indigenous or the Acadians—was encouraged to do so or was particularly welcome in the war effort. Neither group had an inherent place as citizens serving alongside other Canadians. In the end, the situation presents a paradox. On the one hand, that neither group had "belonged" in military service signifies exclusion. Yet, military service also seemed a path to inclusion, to a place in Canadian society, to citizenship. The pieces in this chapter offer diverse views of military history and call on us, as readers, to sit with the complexities and injustices that these histories ask us to confront. Without them, we lose parts of our collective past and truths that shape our society today.

This chapter reminds us how war has marked the Nova Scotian landscape and impacted its communities. Ultimately, the military history of Nova Scotia at war is one of many faces. Each person who has departed Nova Scotia for war or peace efforts—regardless of race or ethnicity and regardless of whether they enlisted, were conscripted, or fought for the right to go to war—had a name, a community, and a story.

Soul of a Nation in the Heart of Halifax

Ken Hynes

Nowhere in Canada has the impact of war been felt so keenly as in Halifax. Since 1749, the city has been home to a large army garrison and, in two world wars, it served as arguably the most important port on the east coast of North America. Between 1914 and 1918, hundreds of thousands of Canadian soldiers and millions of tonnes of cargo were sent overseas to England and on to France and Belgium. On December 6, 1917, the Halifax Explosion rocked the city with the largest man-made blast prior to the dropping of the atomic bomb on Hiroshima in 1945. Almost two thousand people were killed and over nine thousand were injured. Nearly twenty-five thousand citizens were left homeless or forced to live in housing that was severely damaged. The soldiers of the Halifax garrison formed the largest contingent of first responders (five thousand) who did most of the heavy lifting in terms of immediate aid and recovery operations for the community.

During the Second World War, Halifax once again rose to great prominence as a critical convoy marshalling port and the place where over seven hundred thousand Canadian men and women and the majority of war supplies left on the perilous journey across the North Atlantic for England and combat operations in Europe. Halifax was the headquarters for the Royal Canadian Navy, as well as for the Theatre Commander-in-Chief Northwest Atlantic, Canadian Rear Admiral Leonard Murray. Halifax, Dartmouth, Bedford, and the surrounding areas were heavily defended against enemy attack from the air or the sea. The area bristled with fortifications, anti-aircraft guns, searchlights, and a massive anti-submarine net that stretched across the entrance to the harbour.

From these few highlighted examples, there is more than enough evidence to support the statement that all major conflicts of the twentieth century had a significant and lasting impact on our community.

ROLE OF THE ARMY MUSEUM

As the premiere military museum in the Maritimes, the Army Museum Halifax Citadel's mission is to preserve, present, and commemorate the history of Atlantic Canada's soldiers, with a specific emphasis on those from Nova Scotia. The institution strives to provide visitors with the opportunity to learn about those whose service and sacrifice paved the way for the peace and stability that we enjoy today. All were real people with precious lives, hopes, dreams, loves, and aspirations. They were called to do extraordinary things at extraordinary times in our nation's history. Whether they were white, Black, Indigenous, or Acadian, regardless of creed or custom, they stepped forward to fight for peace and freedom and for one another. They opposed tyranny with courage and fortitude, with tens of thousands never to return home. Inside the exhibit spaces of the museum, visitors will see their faces and be able to reach out and touch history.

COMMUNITY OUTREACH

Community outreach and communication have become key elements in the museum's programming to ensure that the unique stories of our soldiers are better known outside the exhibition spaces. From elementary schools to universities, the contribution of our citizen soldiers is not well understood. The First World War was my grandfather's war; the Second World War and the Korean War were those of my father's generation. For many young people today, these conflicts are associated with their great-grandfathers' generation. The further removed we are along the timeline of history, the easier it is to forget about those on whose shoulders we now stand. Peace operations and the war in Afghanistan have more recently re-engaged Canadians, due in part to the impact of enhanced media coverage. The faces of our fallen shown on TV as their bodies travelled the Highway of Heroes on the way to burial emphasized the idea that real sacrifices were made on our behalf. However, a substantial gap in understanding the overall scale of Canada's sacrifice in the past century, as well as the impact that it has had on our development and stature as a nation, is writ large.

While there is plenty of sacred ground on or near the battlefields of France and Belgium, where the majority of our First and Second World Wars' dead were laid to rest, there are sacred and meaningful places right here in our own community for remembrance and commemoration. While not cenotaphs, these places can help us reflect on the concept of selfless service and sacrifice. Providing appropriate human-scaled opportunities for citizens to think about the cost of war is an essential part of the museum's mission: one such example is The Last Steps Memorial Arch.

In August 2016, The Last Steps Memorial Arch was unveiled by the Army Museum at the Halifax waterfront, marking the place where 350,000 Canadians sailed toward an unknown future in Belgium and France during the First World War. Whether a soldier was killed, wounded, or returned home seemingly unscathed, their experiences forever changed them and how they saw the world. The effects on families in the community were no less striking, given the high casualty rate at the front. To symbolize the soldiers' lives, boot prints were branded onto the wharf at the site adjacent to the Maritime Museum of the Atlantic, ending on a gangway leading through the arch, creating a portal of remembrance. In the words of our project artist, Nancy Keating, "Those boot prints were always there, we just couldn't see them." In 2017, the Army Museum installed a companion memorial on the battlefield near Passchendaele, Belgium. At Canada Gate, the boot prints reappear, just a few hundred metres short of Passchendaele Ridge. Those footsteps head in the direction of a place whose name will never be forgotten. More than four thousand

Figure 2. The Last Steps Memorial Arch, Halifax.
(PHOTO BY KEN HYNES)

Canadian soldiers were killed and another twelve thousand were wounded in the Battle of Passchendaele, which has forever linked the people of this country to Belgium and the people of Flanders. These are the kind of community projects that help our citizens connect to their ancestors and their own family history of service to Canada.

More than half of Canada's 67,000 First World War dead lie in Flanders Fields. Another 173,000 were wounded in that conflict. In the Second World War, 45,000 servicemen and -women were killed and 55,000 were wounded. In Korea, there were 516 dead and over 700 wounded. Peace operations have killed 130 and wounded 500 of our men and women, and in Afghanistan, we lost 158, with more than 2,000 returning wounded. The numbers are staggering. However, each statistic has a human face. Each one has a story that adds to the community narrative of service to a cause greater than one's own self-interest. All are worthy of our gratitude and remembrance.

WHY REMEMBER AND COMMEMORATE?

The streets of this city where we walk, drive, or cycle every day have felt hundreds of thousands of footsteps of Canadian servicemen and servicewomen as they departed for and returned home from a conflict. It is here in this community that we must continue to honour them and pay tribute to those who have served in the uniform of our country. There are so many grim statistics that one can hardly come to grips with the staggering numbers when studying the conflicts of the twentieth and twenty-first centuries. From 1914 up until this moment, there have been close to 113,000 Canadian sailors, soldiers, and aviators who have lost their lives, and 231,000 have been wounded in body or mind, or listed as missing.

Every Remembrance Day ceremony, at cenotaphs around the city, we honour the fallen from the First and Second World Wars, the Korean War, peace operations, and the war in Afghanistan. More than a century ago, in the First World War, thirty thousand Nova Scotians volunteered for service overseas and three thousand never came home. Halifax itself was nearly destroyed by an explosion in the First World War. If not for the soldiers of the Halifax garrison and the sailors of the Royal Canadian Navy, Halifax would have suffered even greater harm in the aftermath. A Canadian military doctor remarked that the devastation here was equal to anything he had seen in Flanders. What is the legacy? How do we ensure we don't forget the price that was paid for our freedom?

Beyond Remembrance Day, it's important that we learn from the war experiences of Canada and Nova Scotia, as these have forever changed who we are. Those changes have seen us take on a greater and often costly role in world affairs. Given the losses that our communities have endured in the past century, the old expression "Lest We Forget" is meaningless unless we take action to ensure that our warriors for peace and justice never become merely faded photographs in mouldering frames. We must strive to be worthy of the sacrifice given on our behalf. The murmuring ghosts of tens of thousands still linger on distant battlefields and oceans. As long as we're free, we owe a debt of gratitude that can never fully be repaid. At the very least, we owe them a promise to remember the human cost of war and to never repeat the mistakes that lead to armed conflict. The Army Museum Halifax Citadel continues to try to keep that promise.

We Were There: Remembering Nova Scotia's Mi'kmaw War Veterans

Don Julien and Jenna Stewart

Dr. Don Julien is the executive director of the Confederacy of Mainland Mi'kmaq (1994–present). He is a member of the Order of Canada and the Order of Nova Scotia, both granted for his work promoting Mi'kmaw history, language, and culture. He has spent more than forty years researching and documenting Mi'kmaw history, with his latest project being a forthcoming book devoted to the Mi'kmaq of Nova Scotia who served in the First World War. Jenna Stewart, at the time a student in history and political studies at Mount Saint Vincent University, interviewed Julien to learn more about his journey to tell the stories of Nova Scotia's Mi'kmaw veterans.

JENNA STEWART: Could you please summarize your research about Mi'kmaw war veterans?

DON JULIEN: I was very interested in how our people were handled because we didn't become citizens of our own country until May of 1956. During the First World War, the Department of Indian Affairs was trying to block the entry of First Nations men—mostly men—into the Canadian military because we were wards of the federal government. So, the federal government was to take care of us—not us take care of them. But by the time the order-in-council to exempt First Nations men from conscription was issued and people were notified of it, there were four thousand First Nations people that had joined the Canadian military. The order-in-council wasn't lifted until 1917 when the federal government was running out of volunteers and started conscription.

My interest is to focus on celebrating the lives of the guys that did go over. We had ninety from Nova Scotia, and we lost ten who didn't come home. One died during training in Aldershot, NS, so he was buried in Bear River, but the other nine were overseas and they were buried in different cemeteries there. When I started research in 1970 on land claims and treaty rights, some of these gentlemen were still alive from the First World War. They were elderly, but they were alive. I wish, at that time, I would have had the interest in doing this research because then I would have had first-hand knowledge from the individuals that went over. It would have been a lot better than reading their military files, which I got out of the national archives in Ottawa.

JENNA STEWART: Can you share the story of one of the First Nations men who went to war?

DON JULIEN: The stories were fascinating. A couple of them were exceptional. One was Sam Glode. Sam Glode was decorated with the Distinguished Conduct Medal. He was a trapper and a guide in Nova Scotia. He also worked in pulp mills. As a hunting and fishing guide before the First World War, Sam befriended several wealthy Americans, and he was often asked to visit them in New York and Massachusetts. He also travelled through Newfoundland, and once he took a train across Canada to meet up with a hunting party in Alaska. So, when he came home, he decided that maybe he should join the Canadian military. Sam and three of his brothers joined at the same time. Sam and one of his brothers joined in New Brunswick, and his other two brothers joined in Nova Scotia. They were in two different battalions.

They were waiting to be sent to France, and one of Sam's friends popped his head in the tent while they were waiting there and he said, "Look, ah, we're being mustered out." Sam said, "Well, I'm not an engineer. I'm not a miner." His friend said, "They don't know that; they don't know that you're not. So, you just come out with us, and they'll give you the training."

For their training, they built tunnels from our side of the line almost to the German side, put explosives down, and then came back and watched it blow up. Germans were doing the same thing to us. So, Sam quickly adapted to mining and went from regular army to the engineering corps. At the end of the war, he was assigned to clear land mines and, instead of having his men be in danger, he cleared 450 land mines by himself. So, Sam received the Distinguished Conduct Medal for his actions in clearing land mines. That was one of the higher medals received.

JENNA STEWART: What inspired you to start this research?

DON JULIEN: I formed an Elders' group in 2001 for Mi'kmawey Debert [Cultural Centre]. It's a project to try to get a museum of Mi'kmaw history in place in central Nova Scotia. The idea for this research came from those Elders. They started talking about whether anyone ever did research on the First World War. I said, "No, but I've always been interested in finding out where our guys went, who served, and who served from my community." I started looking at Google and, finally, I found research done in the early 1990s out of British Columbia. I read it and went, "Oh my god, it has just about every one of our guys that served!" The only ones missing were those with the last names Labrador and Meuse for some reason. I mean, this individual, Jeff Schlingloff, was doing research from British Columbia, so he's not going to know the families. So, I started talking to the families of some of the Meuses and Labradors, and I said, "Was there any of your family that served?" and they said "Yes, there were a number of them." I asked them to give me the names and, if they had the birth dates, it would be appreciated.

I've emailed the researcher from British Columbia several times, and I also told him that I was going to be using the information in a book. I expanded my book from Nova Scotia to at least give tribute to New Brunswick, Newfoundland, Prince Edward Island, and Quebec—the Mi'kmaq and the Maliseet [Wolastoqiyik]. So, in my book, I have a list of people. I don't have their files, but it's a tribute list of each person that served from each of the communities in New Brunswick, Quebec, Prince Edward Island, and Newfoundland. I concentrated on Nova Scotia and got their military files from the archives so I could tell each of their stories. Then, while I was doing that, I said, "Well, Schlingloff has a list of Second World War veterans too—126 Second World War vets." I included all their names—those that served in the First and Second World Wars and the Korean conflict from the Atlantic area. So, if someone else at some point in time wants to do the research, they have the names and what communities the veterans were from.

JENNA STEWART: Was the experience of the Mi'kmaw veterans different from that of the non-Indigenous?

DON JULIEN: I guess the enrollment way back then wasn't sophisticated. Well, it wasn't sophisticated in the Second World War, but it was a lot better than in the First World War. People got to meet each other and train with each other and had to rely on each other. So, there was a lot of camaraderie that came out of the First World War. People remember friends and also their sadness in losing friends they had made. It would have opened a lot of doors for friendship. It's not easy being in a war and depending on your buddy next to you, regardless of their race or where they were from. So, I think there was a lot of camaraderie. After the boys came back to Nova Scotia, there was still a bit of camaraderie but not as much as they were hoping. A lot of them went back to their communities—hunted, fished, trapped, and whatever else. Some of them got a better education. Then there were a number of people that went to the US to live because it was a little bit easier to find a job in the States than around here. Boston was the biggest area where our people went after the First World War.

JENNA STEWART: What do you hope that people who read your book, when it is released, will take away from it?

DON JULIEN: What I want is for the kids to realize that our guys fought in the First World War. We didn't have to, but we did. If there are some Mi'kmaw veterans that they can identify with—great-great-grandfathers or someone like that—then at least people will know about them and be very proud of them, and they'll have a book of their names, regimental numbers, and what regiments they served in. That's my biggest thing: that the kids will be aware that we Mi'kmaq weren't just sitting around during the First World War. We were involved. We were involved in the Second World War, too.

JENNA STEWART: Could you please share your insights on the effects of war and peace on the Mi'kmaw communities after the First World War?

DON JULIEN: To serve overseas was prestigious in a way—that the guys were in uniform and were able to send money home to their families. When they came back, a lot basically resumed what they did before the war, and some of them learned how to drive trucks and stuff. So, it benefited us in a sense. The War Veterans Allowance, which was given to veterans who were injured, helped the families a bit and, of course, there was the money they received when they got out. In Pictou Landing, a lot of the guys there bought fishing equipment and, in other areas, people helped build their homes with the money they received. It wasn't a lot of money, but it helped them improve their houses. People became a little bit better educated because they were out in the world seeing what everyone else is doing.

JENNA STEWART: Is there anything else you would like to share?

DON JULIEN: While serving on a peacekeeping tour in Cyprus with the United Nations in 1967, I met a girl in Famagusta, and she wanted to know what nationality I was because I was in the sun, so I was a little darker. She said, "I know you're Canadian, but is there a nationality behind you?" I replied, "Well, yeah, First Nations. I'm an Indian person from Canada."

A lot of people in the 1970s, they did not know too much about Indigenous Peoples. Their idea of an Indian was like John Wayne in the movies. After they would learn who I was, then they wanted to know a lot more about our Mi'kmaw culture. I found that people abroad were more fascinated once they found out I was First Nations than people in Canada. I felt like a celebrity. People were like, "Oh my god, you're a real tried-and-true North American Indian," and I would say, "Yes, I am," and they would go "Wow!" and they would be touching me. And in Norway, it was the same way.

I felt better being who I was overseas than I did at home. Now, thinking about...some of the guys in the First World War, how that must have been for them! People must have been fascinated that there were Indians in the war, and people were probably fascinated with our guys. They were fascinated with me in the 1960s and 1970s, so imagine between 1914 and 1918. Our guys must have been quite the celebrities once people found out who they were. It's amazing how other countries accepted us a bit more than what our own country did. Things have changed; I think they have changed.

Baie Sainte-Marie Goes to War: Experiences of Nova Scotia Acadians, 1916–1921

Gregory Kennedy

Acadian contributions to the Canadian Expeditionary Force (CEF) have received scant attention from historians (Kennedy 2018). Scholars have long noted that French-Canadians in Quebec were less likely to enlist voluntarily, while some publicly opposed the conflict as an example of European imperialism. As recruitment rates fell across the country in 1916, many Anglo-Canadians heaped scorn on the "slackers" who they claimed were not doing their part. The federal imposition of conscription in 1917 intensified linguistic divisions and culminated in the ugly Easter Riots of 1918 in Quebec City. It would be impossible here to summarize the complexity of the crisis and its interminable consequences for national unity. Andrew Theobald captures the essential paradox of the First World War as "both a great Canadian triumph and a costly victory in a brutal war that fractured the basic fabric of the country" (2008, 10).

Francophones in the Maritime provinces had their own views about military service. The Acadians living in Baie Sainte-Marie were part of a larger diaspora created by the deportation of much of the French population from British Nova Scotia beginning in 1755. John Mack Faragher (2006) has characterized this Great Upheaval (*le Grand Dérangement*) as an act of ethnic cleansing, with the forced transportation and deliberate dispersion of a specific ethnic and religious group and with a high mortality rate due to disease, malnutrition, and exposure. The Acadians living in Nova Scotia in 1914 were the descendants of those who had overcome great obstacles to return to their homeland. One might assume, then, that Acadians would show little interest in fighting for Great Britain. In contrast, many Acadian leaders saw military service with the CEF as an opportunity. The outbreak of the First World War coincided with the growth of an Acadian national movement seeking to gain greater recognition within Canadian society. A prominent group of notables including politicians, lawyers, educators, and newspaper editors successfully lobbied the federal government to create an Acadian national battalion in December 1915. They hoped that the newly formed 165th Battalion would highlight the contributions made by Acadian soldiers. With its headquarters in Moncton, the unit established depots in Edmundston, Caraquet, Antigonish, and Meteghan. Our research team has identified nearly twelve hundred Acadian volunteers in the 165th Battalion. While nearly half of them signed up in southeastern New Brunswick, a significant contingent of eighty-six recruits hailed from Baie Sainte-Marie. After the city of Moncton (183), the small town of Meteghan (56) furnished the largest number of soldiers.

The 165th Battalion did not meet the hopes of its founders. Medical exams, desertion, and the release of underage soldiers brought the strength down to about 550 men at the time that the unit went overseas in March 1917. The army transferred most of the volunteers to the Canadian Forestry Corps (CFC). They went to France to cut wood, rather than fight in the trenches. Claude Léger suggests that this may explain why Acadian historians rarely mention the 165th Battalion; it brought "no memorable glory" back home (2001, 209). However, the fate of this unit was similar to others created in the later stages of the war. Across Canada, most of the men who wanted to go had already signed up, and the front line needed reinforcements rather than newly formed units.

PROFILE OF THE BAIE SAINTE-MARIE SOLDIERS IN THE 165TH BATTALION

A noteworthy aspect of the recruitment for the 165th Battalion was the central role played by Émile Jean Stehelin, one of eight brothers, six of whom served in the CEF. The Stehelin family originated in Alsace, a territory ceded to Germany in 1871 and returned to France after the First World War. They moved to Pointe-de-l'Église (Church Point) in 1892 and established a lucrative lumbering operation in the region. Émile was one of the first to respond to the call to form an Acadian national unit and was appointed as the officer in charge of the Meteghan depot. By the end of January 1916, he had recorded thirty-eight enlistments, including several individuals who appear to have worked for his business as woodcutters and sawyers. Despite being too old for war service, Émile was promoted to the rank of major and commanded a forestry company in France.

Like other Francophone recruits, the volunteers from Baie Sainte-Marie tended to be young, unmarried men born in Canada. By comparison, more than half of the soldiers in the CEF were not born in Canada; most were recent immigrants from Great Britain. The Acadians also stand out for the large number of recruits declaring *farming* as their principal occupation (about 40 percent in comparison with just 22 percent for the CEF as a whole) and the near absence of men with previous service (just 3 percent in comparison with 35 percent for the CEF). The 165th Battalion included many young men and adolescents who had moved from homes in rural parishes in search of work in factories or with the railroad. On a smaller scale, a similar trend emerged in Baie Sainte-Marie, with men from several communities already having moved to work in Meteghan (Duguid 1935, 35; Gagnon 1986, 319–364; Morton 1993, 62–63).

Some of the volunteers lied about their age in order to enlist. Linking them to their records in the 1911 Canadian census (or the 1910 American census) helps confirm the situation. A closer look at some of the soldiers who were younger than eighteen or older than forty-five not only reveals a particular motivation to serve but also considerable mobility. We tend to assume that the inhabitants of small rural parishes were sedentary, but in fact, employment and family networks could extend beyond provincial and international boundaries. For example, Charles Deveau of Mavillette was just thirteen years old when he signed up, claiming to be eighteen. The son of a ship carpenter, Charles had been born in the US in 1902 and only moved back to Nova Scotia in 1907. Charles went overseas with the 165th Battalion. Meanwhile, François Dugas of Meteghan, who was only fourteen years old when he enlisted, was released as underage around Christmas 1916. François was also born in the US, and his mother was born in Quebec. On the other side of the age spectrum, George Deveau claimed to be forty-three, but was in fact forty-nine years old. He was originally from Yarmouth but had recently moved to Meteghan. According to the 1911 Census, George was a modest fisherman, but in his attestation paper, he claimed to be a firefighter and to have two years of previous service with the Argentine navy.

The case of four brothers, born and raised in Meteghan, who enlisted together, is representative of many local conditions. Joseph (twenty-eight), William (twenty-one), Paul (twenty), and Frank (eighteen) Saulnier enlisted with the 112th (Nova Scotia) Battalion and transferred into the 165th Battalion in the spring of 1916. Although three of the brothers claimed to be farmers, a look at the 1911 Census reveals that their father, Hilaire, owned a fishing boat and they worked with him. The entire family included thirteen people: Hilaire and Rose, their ten children, and Mary Saulnier, Hilaire's elderly aunt. Hilaire brought in just $300 annually in 1911, while Joseph and William declared a combined income of $330 for thirty-six weeks of work at sea. Their sister Elizabeth worked fifty-two weeks a year, sixty hours a week as a domestic servant, bringing in an additional $100 (Emery et al. 2002, 115–137). Desmond Morton argues that the military daily salary of $1.10, plus a separation allowance of

$20 each month, as well as room and board, would have been a clear economic incentive for families like the Sauldniers (2004, 32).

The four Saulnier brothers had different experiences of the war. William was one of many Canadian men ultimately rejected for service in the CEF due to physical difficulties. The doctor's report indicates that he "complains of pain and difficulty in walking any distance. Pain in both knees and shoulder" and that the disability was pre-existing and likely permanent. The file also indicates that William got married to a local woman named Lizzie sometime in 1917. The oldest brother, Joseph, appears to have done well in uniform, being promoted to the rank of sergeant while serving with the 47th Company of the 5th District of the CFC. Most of the 165th Battalion soldiers who went overseas ultimately ended up in the 5th District, stationed in the Jura region of France near the Swiss border. His file also relates that Joseph spent ten days in the hospital after suffering a gunshot wound near his right ear in May 1918. Since his company did not experience combat, something else must have happened. The fact that there was no comment in the file, no disciplinary action, report of an investigation, or further medical follow-up suggests an accident, but the incident serves as a reminder that even while cutting wood this was still a military organization with a certain amount of risk. Paul joined Joseph in the 47th Company but was in and out of hospital with a hernia and, later, a crushed finger. Paul received a good-conduct badge but did not advance beyond the rank of private. Both Joseph and Paul would have come home with scars they would bear for the rest of their lives. Frank, the youngest brother, found himself separated from his siblings in the 39th Company, but still with other Acadians and located in the same area. Frank also spent some time in the hospital, one of many soldiers to be afflicted with the Spanish flu in late 1918. The 5th District routine orders describe the influenza working its way through camp as "severe and highly infective" (Library and Archives Canada, n.d.).

The three Saulnier brothers in the CFC worked hard and faced their share of adversity while overseas. After the Armistice, they had to wait several months for their turn to go home. Frank arrived in Halifax in early March 1919, while Paul returned last in July, travelling through Saint John, NB.

RETURN TO CIVILIAN SOCIETY

Few scholars have studied the demobilization and reintegration process of returning CEF soldiers. The most notable exception is Desmond Morton, who has described how ill-prepared the government was for the massive task of supporting veterans and their families. Pensions were rare and given only for a proven disability attributable to military service. Widows or widowed mothers of those killed in military service also received modest sums. Financial support for mental illness was nearly unthinkable. Morton affirms that most returning Canadian soldiers found themselves struggling with poverty (2004, 157).

Finding soldiers in the 1921 Canadian or 1920 American censuses provides a crucial snapshot of how they were doing after the war. We can also consult ship passenger lists and border control documents to find veterans moving around. As we have seen, there were existing networks that connected families in Baie Sainte-Marie to their kin in other parts of the Maritime provinces, in Quebec, and in the US. It is not surprising, then, that some of the former soldiers chose to move away from home. In 1921, three of the eighty-six Acadian soldiers from this region had died, forty-eight were living in Canada, and twenty more had moved to the US. The fifteen veterans who could not be found may have died, changed their names, been in transit, or simply been missed by the census takers. Of those who could be found and were still living (sixty-eight individuals), 30 percent had left the country, most ending up in Massachusetts. This was a much higher rate of mobility than that observed before the war. Three men stand out as they decided to continue soldiering for the Americans. In an exceptional case, the 1920 census recorded Iréné Comeau at Camp

Gaillard, a marine base in Panama. Frank, the youngest Saulnier brother, was among those who crossed the international border in 1919. He must have still been on the move in 1920, as our next sign of him is in the 1930 US census, living in Whitman, Massachusetts. Frank married in the early 1920s and had two small children by that time.

Before the war, almost all of the volunteers were single; after the war, approximately half of them married quickly. William Saulnier, as noted, married while training with the army. After his discharge, he settled as a farmer and by 1921 had two children, Lea and Edward. Although the enumerator listed William as the head of household, the young family lived with Lizzie's mother and likely relied on her help, given William's physical disability. The other volunteers returned home to live with parents or other family members. This was the case for Joseph and Paul Saulnier; Joseph picked up right where he had left off before the war, helping his father on the boat. However, the census indicates that father and son had been unemployed for two months, reflecting the seasonal nature of the work. Paul, on the other hand, made just a hundred dollars working as a labourer. Living at home helped him get by while he searched for better employment.

CONCLUSION

Acadian Nova Scotians joined up for many of the same reasons as their Anglophone counterparts. Many wanted to do their part for Canada, and some saw the CEF as an attractive employment option. Of course, there was a particular push to support the 165th Battalion, the Acadian national unit, led by local notables including Émile Jean Stehelin. We should remember that despite their difficult history of deportation, resettlement, and marginalization as a linguistic minority, many of the Baie Sainte-Marie Acadians proved willing to enlist. As with all Canadian battalions, some of the volunteers were underage or medically unfit and did not go overseas. Those who did found themselves cutting woods in old-growth forests of France, rather than in the trenches. While this ensured that most of them came home, many would be disappointed that they did not have the opportunity to fight. Some of those restless souls quickly moved on after returning home, while others struggled to establish themselves. They had missed several crucial years in the typical life course of a young person, and it would take some time to catch up. Many CEF veterans struggled with poverty after the war. The minority status of the Baie Sainte-Marie Acadians further marginalized them even as it connected them through a common unit experience.

Chapter 6

Halifax Explosion

Introduction

Barbara Lounder

The December 1917 explosion in Halifax Harbour is referred to as the Halifax Explosion, though this belies the fact that it affected a much larger area than just the city. The collision of two ships, one filled with explosives, took place in the waters of the Narrows (Kepe'k) in Halifax Harbour (Kjipuktuk), with the ensuing catastrophic detonation taking place next to Pier 6 in the neighbourhood of Richmond (l'-ntauimk), on the west shore of the city's harbour. The surrounding communities and neighbourhoods of the Halifax peninsula (Kuowa'qamikt), Dartmouth (Punamu'kwati'jk), and the area around the Bedford Basin (Asoqmapskiajk) were all affected.

WHAT HAPPENED AT KEPE'K ON THE MORNING OF DECEMBER 6, 1917?

At approximately 8:45 A.M. on December 6, 1917, the SS *Imo* and the SS *Mont-Blanc* collided in the Narrows of Halifax Harbour. The collision was the result of a number of circumstances: the *Mont-Blanc*, loaded with a heavy cargo of benzol, TNT, gun cotton, picric acid, and other explosives intended for use on the First World War battlefields, had arrived at the entrance of the harbour later than expected on December 5, after the submarine nets had been set in place for the night. The *Mont-Blanc* moored off McNabs Island overnight and made its way into the harbour under the direction of Harbour Pilot Francis Mackey the next morning. Mackey was one of the few people who knew of the dangerous cargo onboard. As the vessel headed south toward the Bedford Basin, where it was to have joined a convoy heading to Europe, it encountered several other ships including the SS *Imo*, which had been chartered by the Commission for Relief in Belgium and was being brought south through the harbour by pilot William Hayes. Following a series of miscommunications and other errors, the *Mont-Blanc* and the *Imo* collided mid-harbour, and the resulting sparks ignited the benzol on the deck of the munitions ship.

The vessels disengaged following the collision, and the disabled *Imo* drifted east toward Dartmouth while the crew of the *Mont-Blanc*, who knew of the deadly cargo, abandoned their blazing ship and rowed their lifeboats across the harbour. They reached safety on the Dartmouth side, disembarking at the Mi'kmaw settlement of Turtle Grove and running for cover. The *Mont-Blanc* wedged itself alongside the wharf at Pier 6 on the Halifax waterfront and exploded at 9:04:35 A.M. The resulting blast wave, tsunami, and fires that raged through Richmond and the surrounding neighbourhoods killed almost two thousand people and injured nine thousand more, most of them civilians. Thousands of homes and businesses were destroyed. It was the largest human-made explosion until nuclear weapons were used to destroy Hiroshima and Nagasaki in 1945 (Bean et al. 2017).

The explosion was transformative in shaping Halifax's urban core, with neighbourhoods and areas such as Mulgrave Park, Needham Hill, the Hydrostone District, the Cogswell Interchange, Africville, and Shannon Park created or profoundly altered by the event and its aftermath. And what became of Richmond? It was effectively erased. While the area was eventually redeveloped, the neighbourhood is no longer known by the same name. Indeed, erasure and absence have been a conspicuous part of the post-explosion legacy all along.

A STORY OF WAR AND PEACE

The historical narratives of the Halifax Explosion are stories of war and conflict, militarism, and survival, just as surely as are the accounts from the First World War battlefields of Europe. A horrendous disaster and a tragedy of grotesque proportions, it was intrinsically connected to the war and to the longer history of militarization of Halifax Harbour and British colonization in general. The result of a relatively minor collision between two vessels, the explosion was anything but an accident. Given wartime secrecy and propagandizing by governments and the press, bureaucratic ineptitude, and the practice of transporting deadly munitions through civilian communities, it was a disaster waiting to happen.

The 2017 centenary of the Halifax Explosion provided an important occasion for revisiting historical accounts and bringing new information and perspectives forward. It allowed for reflection on political and civic power and inequities, and on militarism. It also offered an opportunity for envisioning a future in which such disasters are impossible. Because very few explosion survivors are still living, the centenary marked the passing of this event from personal experience to historical accounts and narratives. Important questions about public memory and commemoration are central in this process.

Disaster narratives help establish a sense of place and belonging. Stories of traumatic events affecting a specific geographic area and multiple communities—like those of the Halifax Explosion—are incomplete, sometimes contradictory, and evolve over time. As aspects of a living history, they are different in each telling; new, disputed, or amended stories should not be dismissed as revisionism or rewriting, but listened to and examined because they demonstrate that knowledge is always incomplete, as realities are diverse and experienced through different lenses.

Research on the Halifax Explosion has been detailed and varied and includes the work of Janet Kitz, who began with unpacking the abandoned mortuary bags containing personal effects of unnamed victims, and her careful efforts, over many years, to find out who these people were, what happened to them, and how survivors and descendants were linked to them (Kitz 1989). Other researchers and writers such as Alan Ruffman and Colin D. Howell (1994), Joel Zemel (2014), Janet Maybee (2015), and Ken Cuthbertson (2017) have followed. While research can help in understanding events, stories of heroic rescue, relief, and rebuilding efforts are also important wartime and disaster narratives that can help in understanding and coping with immense suffering and loss. Janet Maybee's research on the role that Truro citizens played in the hours and days immediately following the explosion corrects many of the assumptions about who provided the first relief efforts. The inequities of the Halifax Explosion relief efforts are clear to us a century later, and the misogyny, racism, classism, and other biases of social work and charity are covered by Michelle Hébert (2007), Jacob Remes (2016), and David Sutherland (2017).

The losses of Indigenous and African Nova Scotian communities in the disaster and its aftermath continue to remain little known. Knowledge keepers, historians, artists, and activists in these communities continue to discover and share important information about Mi'kmaw and Black Nova Scotian experiences of the explosion. In addition, the stories of midwives, expectant mothers, and many other women are only now being told; accounts of miscarriages, stillbirths, and premature deliveries feature in Ami McKay's writing (2006) and in Xara Choral Theatre's centenary production, *The Hours Turn to Nothing*. Some of the stories of fractured and relocated families—the internal refugees of the explosion—are just being pieced together now, in some cases by descendants; however, accurate records are difficult to locate, with names misspelled and women's names not always recorded.

ARTISTS AND THE EXPLOSION

Artists have also helped to document the living history of the explosion by creating important depictions and chronicles of the events, and they continue to do so today. In 1917, artist Arthur Lismer, along with photographers and journalists of the day, made many of the most important visual records of the devastation. In 1977, artists Graham Metson and Cheryl Lean organized *The Halifax Explosion: December 6, 1917*, an exhibition of documentary photographs and other materials from the explosion. These, along with Metson's book of the same name (1978), were the first efforts, sixty years after the explosion, to provide a record of and to reflect on the visual images associated with the events.

During the centenary year, one of the most compelling cultural explorations of the explosion was Zuppa Theatre's *At This Hour: A Deposition of Harbour Pilot Francis Mackey*. This theatre production was a verbatim performance of excerpts from the Wreck Commissioner's inquiry, the legal investigation that took place immediately following the explosion. The production, inspired by Maybee's work, took place in the very same room of the Halifax Court House on Spring Garden Road that the inquiry had used.

Not only have artists used a variety of media to record and reflect on the explosion, but they have also used a range of contemporary approaches and technologies to present new information and insights, including a mobile app, Drifts, created by Narratives in Space+Time Society (NiS+TS), and The Psychogeographer's Table, a collaboration between NiS+TS and GEM Lab that used LIDAR mapping, CNC milling, and augmented reality. In addition, Halifax Regional Municipality acknowledged the centenary with Halifax Explosion commemorative markers at key locations, these being iconic laser-cut steel structures designed by Rayleen Hill Architecture + Design.

WHAT IS LEFT TO SAY ABOUT THE EXPLOSION?

The three contributions in this chapter focus on the 2017 centenary of the Halifax Explosion as an occasion for different communities (local, national, and international) to remember the wartime disaster and to reflect on questions about commemoration and public memory. Designer John deWolf describes the process of redesign for Fort Needham Memorial Park, including important stages of community consultation and historical research, and his creative exploration of topography, vistas, and materials as tools for telling explosion stories. Catherine Martin, Juanita Peters, and Paige Farah engage in a poignant and powerful exchange of what the explosion means to them now, a hundred years later, from perspectives deeply informed by knowledge and experience of racism, colonization, and class oppression. Artists Robert Bean and Angela Henderson write about the work that NiS+TS has done using architectural models of buildings related to the explosion as part of their larger project "Walking the Debris Field of the Halifax Explosion."

WHY THE HALIFAX EXPLOSION MATTERS TODAY

Over a century later, there is still much to learn about the Halifax Explosion. Shrapnel from the *Mont-Blanc*, broken glass, "black rain," diaries, letters, and photographs continue to be discovered. Unmarked graves are still to be located, and mortuary bags containing personal effects remain unclaimed. Some of the basic facts of the disaster are still being established. For example, the official list of the dead is still being revised as new information comes to light. The list, maintained by the Nova Scotia Archives, currently includes 1,782 names. As the harbour was a site of migration for thousands of military personnel, sailors, and civilians from around the world during wartime, the list may never be completely accurate.

If there is much to learn about the explosion, there is even more to uncover about the risk of another disaster in the future. Kjipuktuk continues to be a highly militarized site. With much of the waterfront occupied by Department of National Defence facilities and the Irving Halifax Shipyard, Halifax Harbour is at the centre of a new era of militarism. This use of a natural resource is generally regarded as benign, if not an outright benefit; the promise of good jobs and other economic benefits is persuasive to many. Despite the knowledge of the loss and suffering caused by the 1917 explosion, there is little public discussion of the dangers associated with the decisions, policies, and practices around the militarized use of the harbour today. We must ask, could a disaster of similar proportions happen today?

Resolve and Rebirth: The Narrative Environment of Fort Needham Memorial Park

John deWolf

As Barbara Lounder has noted, the Halifax Explosion caused unprecedented death, injury, and destruction and dramatically changed the history of a city and a country. The years following the tragedy led to changes in commercial and naval traffic control, the establishment of the Canadian National Institute for the Blind, and a city reimagined and rebuilt. One of the positive outcomes was the development of Fort Needham Memorial Park. Ceded to the City of Halifax in 1942 by the Halifax Relief Commission in remembrance of the victims of the 1917 Halifax Explosion, the 63,000-square-metre (15.6-acre) Fort Needham Memorial Park is one of the largest public open spaces in the city. In addition to its commemorative function, it is an active park providing recreation and green space for residents from the surrounding neighbourhoods.

COMMUNITY

"When Britain is at war, Canada is at war. There is no distinction," Prime Minister Sir Wilfrid Laurier declared in 1910. But the First World War, when it came, churned on, and neither Laurier nor his successor, Sir Robert Borden could have predicted the profound consequences of it in Canada, particularly those of December 6, 1917, in Halifax. At the time, Halifax had a population of over fifty thousand people, including about five thousand soldiers present in support of the war effort (Armstrong 2005; Government of Canada 2019). In the blink of an eye, the explosion wiped the community of Richmond from the face of the city. About two thousand people—one in twenty-five—died; one in five suffered injuries, and one in ten were left without a place to live. While there are no longer any remaining human witnesses to the tragedy, the Memorial Park on Fort Needham Hill, with its vantage point overlooking ground zero of the explosion, will forever be tied to that devastating event.

For decades, the park suffered from a loss of focus from its original purpose as a regional park and failed to fully convey the significance of the Halifax Explosion and its impact on the city and country. In 2014, Halifax Regional Municipality commissioned a team with the purpose of improving the site's commemoration of the 1917 Halifax Explosion and creating a signature regional park in Halifax's North End.[1] Extensive community discussions and research led to a master plan for the park which balances interpretation, ceremony, and recreation.

In 2016, the project moved from master plan to implementation, with two teams of designers led by Sandra Cooke and myself to realize the park's potential as both a commemorative site and a neighbourhood park. A primary challenge was to provide information about the explosion while ensuring that the park met the needs of the surrounding community. The solution was an interdisciplinary approach that resulted in integrating interpretive information into the landscape.

There were, however, countless stories to draw from for inclusion in the interpretive information.[2] The history of Needham Hill goes back to the settlement of Halifax in 1749 and a 323,749-square-metre (80-acre) land grant for the Governor's North Farm. Like Citadel Hill—the heart of Halifax around which the city was planned—Needham Hill offered a strategic defensive command of Halifax Harbour and especially the Narrows, the gateway to one of the finest ice-free harbours in North America.

Needham Hill, therefore, also has a long-standing military history. Initially cleared for agriculture, the site was quickly seized as defence for the Royal Naval Dockyard in 1776 when an earthen redoubt, barracks, and later, a blockhouse were constructed. As the city expanded around the hill, by the time of Confederation, the space was well-used by the Richmond neighbourhood for community, light industry, recreation, and military training.

From an interpretive planning perspective, there was much to draw on. From a user's point of view, it was important to focus the narratives on a few key topics. "Is this a story the hill could tell?" was a question constantly posed by the research team, thus limiting the interpretation primarily to the site. The historical geography of Fort Needham Memorial Park informs its division into two areas or precincts. The southern and western ends overlook a city rebuilt, and the northern and eastern stretches command views of the harbour, the explosion's ground zero and most devastated area. The two areas made for a clear division of interpretive content: the southern end is better suited to interpreting former uses of the site and its geography, while the western edge overlooks the rebuilt portion of the city, leaving the rest of the site to interpret the catastrophe. The two precincts also represent two distinct periods. One is about the ongoing settlement of Halifax over time, and the other is about a catastrophe at a single point in time. In short, the north precinct is about memorializing an event and its aftermath, and the south precinct will—when funding is approved—interpret the site.

Interpretive planning uses themes to unify content and an overarching context through which all interpretation is organized and which holds the visitor experience together. The central message that connects these themes must answer the question, "What aspect of the visit to Fort Needham Memorial Park do you want to resonate with visitors?" As planners and designers, we often organize our work around a core concept. Based on the profile of the Halifax Explosion Memorial Bell Tower, which was built on the site in 1984, the core idea for Fort Needham Memorial Park can be described as "community (equilibrium), loss (disruption), resolve (resolution), and rebirth (new equilibrium)." Summarized as "Resolve and Rebirth," the phrase is encapsulated in the following central message:

> *At 9:05 A.M., on December 6, 1917, a wartime Canadian city endured a devastating explosion: rescued, re-imagined, and rebuilt, Halifax, Nova Scotia, rose anew.*

LOSS

The morning of December 6, 1917, was like any other for the working-class neighbourhood of Richmond: children were in school, mothers returned to their homes, shops began opening for business, and those not called to duty were at work when the explosion occurred at the foot of Richmond Street, directly downhill from where the bell tower stands today in Fort Needham Memorial Park. The entire neighbourhood east of Fort Needham was obliterated. While the hill deflected some of the blast upwards, the force was so strong that even the neighbourhoods in the western shadow of the drumlin were not spared (Kitz and Payzant 2015, 25). Prior to the explosion, Richmond had been a vibrant community, though its industries were experiencing inevitable change. However, according to researcher Suzanne Morton, "What deindustrialization began, the 1917 explosion completed. It removed much physical evidence that industry had ever existed in Richmond" (1990, 46).

The lost neighbourhood of Richmond is now reborn—if only as a staircase in the new park that ascends from Union Street to the bell tower. Precast concrete steps contain letter fragments forming the word R-I-C-H-M-O-N-D and reveal this name to those standing at the bottom of the park. As the visitor ascends, the letterforms fragment and dissipate, like the community once known as Richmond. From the top looking down, the name is not visible at all.

Following the explosion and subsequent tsunami, a "black rain" of shard-ridden debris and unconsumed explosives fell to earth. The stair railing commemorates institutions and organizations that did not return in the wake of the explosion; the vertical parts of the railing are styled as if shards of warped steel had rained down upon the earth, each punctured with the name of a lost school, church, or business. Here, interpretation does not consist of wordy, didactic panels of lengthy prose, but rather of elements in the landscape evocative of the post-explosion events.

Once in the main park area, further powerful but subtle installations let visitors contemplate the 1917 explosion at their own pace and in their own style. The existing Halifax Explosion Memorial Bell Tower has been integrated into the design at the centre of several pivotal interpretive elements. Vince Coleman's last Morse code message—sent to stop an approaching train and saving the lives of hundreds of passengers—has been preserved in the light shield at the base of the bell tower. The rhythmic sequences of dits and dahs are now commemorated in fixed dot-and-dash perforations in weathered steel.

The two ships involved in the initial collision are represented with steel retaining walls matching the length of each ship, one on either side of the main pathway. For each, the ship's bow—matching its direction on the day—is inscribed with the boat's specifications, each stern inscribed with that ship's fate. Along the wall representing the SS *Mont-Blanc*, wooden slats of park benches list the explosive materials in the ship's manifest. A wooden plaque refers to SS *Imo*'s purpose in 1917, a relief ship for neutral Belgium.

The works above are all permanent and spatial, but the design team also choreographed one temporal addition—a light show projecting onto the bell tower. Flashes of solid white and red light and undulating coloured waves convey a twenty-minute story of the explosion on the concrete surface. The light show is visible at night from many points around the city, but best experienced on site.

Figure 3. Richmond Staircase Anamorphic Stair, HRM Fort Needham Memorial Park.
(PHOTO BY SCOTTY SHERIN)

Figure 4. Commemorative Date Wall, HRM Fort Needham Memorial Park.
(PHOTO BY SCOTTY SHERIN)

RESOLVE AND REBIRTH

Today, interpretative media at memorial sites is moving away from the use of didactic panels with an image of a site or object and accompanying text. Instead, the approach is to inspire discovery and further investigation. For example, at Fort Needham Memorial Park, the upper half of one memorial wall of text is perforated and light, while the lower half uses rivets of steel to complete the text as if below a waterline. The only image employed on-site is a digital photographic wrap portraying the destruction and the rebuilding of the surrounding community, which is used to disguise an electrical box.

In addition to the interpretive elements that have been added throughout, the park landscape itself has been vastly improved through topographic modifications, accessible pathways, better connectivity and circulation, new low-maintenance planting, and the creation of a proper gathering space at the bell tower for hosting the annual December 6 ceremony. The site's design preserves and enhances the urban forest, which itself is a testament to the post-explosion rebuilding efforts and regeneration of the city. One hundred years ago, the hill was bare, and today a significant portion of the park is forested.

The success of the Fort Needham Memorial Park project is the result of a strong collaboration between landscape architects, experiential graphic designers, interpretive planners, craftspeople, and the Halifax Regional Municipality, and represents one of the first contemporary park redevelopments of its kind and scale in Atlantic Canada.

NOTES

1 The team included Fathom Studio (then Ekistics Planning + Design and Form:Media), Davis MacIntyre & Associates, archaeologists, and urban forester Dr. Peter Duinker. Ekistics' Rob LeBlanc and Devin Segal were design leads.

2 Using the master plan of Segal and Leblanc, Adam Fine developed the interpretive framework, which aided deWolf, Fine, and Cooke in identifying potential stories and assigning locations and potential storytelling media.

My Explosion

Catherine Martin, Juanita Peters, and Paige Farah, with Barbara Lounder

In October 2016, a group of community activists, artists, and researchers gathered in Halifax for a two-day symposium, "Toward Explosion 2017: Perspectives on the Centenary of the Halifax Explosion,"[1] *in order to explore ways in which the centenary of the disaster might be marked in the most meaningful ways. At a session entitled "My Explosion," Catherine Martin, Juanita Peters, and Paige Farah spoke of their connections to the event. What follows is based on that session: a conversation with Martin about her great-aunt Rachel's memories of the explosion, a spoken word poem by Peters, and reflections by Farah on growing up near ground zero.*

CATHERINE MARTIN

Martin is a Mi'kmaw Elder and independent filmmaker, playwright, storyteller and drummer, and a member of the Millbrook First Nation community. She held the Nancy's Chair in Women's Studies at Mount Saint Vincent University from 2015 to 2017, and in 2017 was appointed to the Order of Canada.

BARBARA LOUNDER: Catherine, thank you for sharing your story about what happened to your family and community at Turtle Grove, or Tufts Cove, during the explosion. Why is this an important story for you?

CATHERINE MARTIN: I feel that I have been guided by my ancestors to tell the story. It goes back to the explosion, but maybe even further. This is a journey that I've been on to get in touch with my great-grandad Joe Cope, and it's been going on my whole life (and probably before).

There are some important places in this story, and one is on Nivens Avenue in Dartmouth, where it comes down the hill and crosses what we know today as India Street. In 1917, it was called Indian Street, and there were two schools nearby. Toward Albro Lake was the Tufts Cove School, which was for the settlers, and then further toward the shore was the Indian School, where children from our family had to go.

My great-grandma Sarah was living in Turtle Grove with her daughter Mary (my grandma), and Mary's brothers and sisters Henry, Rachel, Frank, Leo, Mathilda, and baby Annie. My great-aunt Rachel and my great-uncle Henry and their cousin Louis Copes were on their way to school there when the explosion happened. This is where my great-uncle Henry died, along with his cousin Louis Cope. Louis died right away, and Henry died a little after. Five members of the Cope family are listed in the record of the dead. My great-aunt Rachel was injured, and she passed out at the school. The story about what happened was told by Rachel in a 1946 family interview; the notes from this interview were found a few years ago and shared with me.

BARBARA LOUNDER: How much of what happened did Rachel remember when she gave the interview in 1946?

CATHERINE MARTIN: Rachel, Louis, and Henry were running up Nivens's hill to the school. Rachel talked about seeing the two ships collide, and then the fire. She said that "for an instant the town of Richmond seemed to shimmer like a reflection in a still pond and then everything went black" (Jones 2017). She said that they heard the explosion, and that's the last thing that she could remember. She was knocked out, and the next thing she remembered was waking up a couple of days later, lying on a door and being carried, probably to Windsor Junction.

They were making their way to their winter home and going to get medical help. Rachel said she woke up while she was being carried.

It was snowing, and there was a woman walking beside her, singing a song in Gaelic to comfort her. That's what she remembered. I was told that Rachel didn't talk very often about what happened, so I am very thankful to have been shown that record from the interview with her in 1946.

BARBARA LOUNDER: What happened to the other children?

CATHERINE MARTIN: The others had burns from the fires that broke out when burning chunks of metal rained down. My great-grandma Sarah and her baby Annie, who was badly burned, were taken to a hospital, probably in Kentville (maybe even to the sanatorium there) to recover from their injuries. They recovered from their burns but died from the flu within a year. Frank, who was three, was also badly burned and died three months after the explosion.

BARBARA LOUNDER: How do you feel when you are at Turtle Grove now?

CATHERINE MARTIN: This is really a special place, although now it's very disrupted with the Nova Scotia Power Station at Tufts Cove.

BARBARA LOUNDER: You have woven many parts of this story together in a play that you wrote and perform in.

CATHERINE MARTIN: The play is called *Picking Up the Pieces* and, in it, I have the persona of Rachel, and I am telling the story to my granddaughter, Douzay. It's an emotional experience that is part of my journey to understand my ancestors. The play was part of a photo-based exhibition at the Art Gallery of Nova Scotia called *Kepe'kek: from the Narrows of the Great Harbour,* and I also did it at Shannon Park Elementary School.

BARBARA LOUNDER: In the play, you and Douzay are weaving baskets while you tell the story of Rachel, Henry, and Louis. And you sing a song.

CATHERINE MARTIN: The song is one that came to me and led me to find a lot of things out about my great-grandparents. The lyrics are by Mary Louise Martin, my sister.

"Basketmaker"

Basketmaker, basketmaker
Old woman with the laughing brown in your eyes
Sinewy, leathery hands
So strongly defined
The basketmaker, basketmaker, basketmaker
Own keeper of time
Wisqoq, wisqoq, wisqoq
Basketmaker, basketmaker
You have the heart of a fawn
And any child would see
You are the mystery of dawn
What thoughts have you as you sit so silently
Making works of wooden lines
Weaving my basket up and down, in and out, all around
My basket so fine
Wisqoq, wisqoq, wisqoq
Basketmaker, basketmaker
Old woman with the laughing brown in your eyes
Sinewy, leathery hands
So strongly defined
The basketmaker, basketmaker, basketmaker
Own keeper of time

BARBARA LOUNDER: Is basketmaking something that connects you directly with this story about your family and the explosion?

CATHERINE MARTIN: My great-grandfather Joe Cope was a basketmaker, and his wife Sarah was most likely also one. Like many of the Mi'kmaq who lived in Tufts Cove and other villages near there, they used to spend their time making baskets and peddling them at the Halifax Farmers' Market. This was a good place to be able to sell and trade their products.

They made baskets for harvesting crops, fishing baskets, decorative fancy baskets, as well as hoops for lobster traps and schooner sails, axe handles, clothesline props, birch-bark canoes, and hockey sticks, all from raw materials, especially black ash and maple. The harbour and surrounding waterways were rich with fish and other foods for the Mi'kmaq.

JUANITA PETERS

A gifted storyteller, Peters is a playwright, director, and actor, and worked in broadcast radio and television for many years. She is the general manager of the Africville Museum and a lecturer at the Fountain School of Performing Arts at Dalhousie University.

BARBARA LOUNDER: Juanita, you have deep family roots in this region, going back to some of the earliest and most renowned Black Loyalists, including Thomas Peters and Rose Fortune. This is an important legacy that comes from a history of oppression and hardship, and also from incredible resilience and achievement. Tell us how this shaped your approach to the topic of "My Explosion."

JUANITA PETERS: Very few things that I've ever done in my life were orchestrated by design. They usually came to me because, for some reason, I couldn't not do them. We come to the work not by choice, and so it felt very appropriate to give this spoken word piece to you today.

"My Explosion"

My explosion was not one big bang from a ship in the harbour, you see
But a series of knock-knock-knocks from my family.
A series of knock-knock-knocks from a place beyond my dreams,
a series of knock-knock-knocks that I have no idea from where they came.

My explosion did not include nurses, soldiers, doctors, and the like,
but a sense of loneliness as we ran for our lives.
A sense of loss as we left what was buried in the night.

My explosion came like a rapid and destroyed all that I held dear.
It came fast and furious before I could think and hear
of all the warnings being sent from north to south and throughout the networks
where all the help was about.
It came before I knew what I had, and had to lose,
it came before I could pick up what I had put down.
It made a mess of what grounded me.
It delivered anguish, uncertainty, and pain.
It delivered it far beyond that day, but throughout my life I came to realize
my explosion revealed the history I now claim.

My explosion was not one big bang from a ship in the harbour, you see,
but a series of knock-knock-knocks from my family.
It came to remind me that we had been here long before
and have endured more than the ripping of bricks and woods.
We have been ripped from land and loves
and lost more of what makes us whole
than what can be replaced by any store
or lost in any storm.

They came to remind me that my ancestor Thomas Peters
risked his life for the land my family live and thrive on today.
That Rose Fortune made something out of nothing,
and no one could say either had it easy, in any way.

They knocked to tell me that strength is in the mind and in the soul
and will only grow old fast
if we can't see beyond the mess that often sits in front.

So look behind, and look ahead
and make statues out of the dirt that is left,
and remind yourself of all the most important things you've been told.

My explosion was not one big bang from a ship in the harbour, you see,
But a series of knock-knock-knocks from my family.

PAIGE FARAH

Farah is a social entrepreneur who grew up in the North End of Halifax, not far from Mulgrave Park and ground zero. In 2014, Farah founded a social enterprise called Progress in the Park and initiated programs such as the community garden in Mulgrave Park. In 2019, she was chosen to be a member of the Future City Builders youth cohort in Halifax, where she worked on a project addressing housing insecurity.

BARBARA LOUNDER: Paige, ground zero of the explosion was not far from where you grew up, and not far from neighbourhoods that were rebuilt as part of the Halifax Relief Commission's plan to provide new housing for those who had lost their homes in the explosion. Has your experience growing up in this part of Halifax been important to your sense of community?

PAIGE FARAH: Yes, I relate to the explosion through my experience in the present, living in the North End. I'd like to talk about that through some storytelling and a little opinion.

I've always sucked at remembering birthdays, even of those close to me; however, I did always remember my stepbrother's birthday—December 6—because, to quote my oversimplifying younger self, that was the day that two ships got a little too close and Halifax went *boom* and now we send a Christmas tree to Boston. Not to make light of the two thousand deaths, nine thousand injuries, sixteen hundred homes that were lost, and the nearly twenty-five thousand people left without shelter in the city that literally went up in smoke and flames. But what I find remarkable (and how I choose to find solace in the disaster) are the efforts of those who came together to rebuild the city. That has been the humbling cornerstone of my and many others' first lessons in giving selflessly.

I grew up in the North End of Halifax and have had my admiration for the city directly shaped by its history of tragedy and rebuilding. Three years ago, I started an initiative that helped build a community garden in the heart of what was once ground zero of the Halifax Explosion, Mulgrave Park, in the area formerly known as Richmond.

And I find that there's something serendipitous and poetic about being able to build something that, in its material form, is its own little ecosystem and is emblematic of a community coming together to produce something—produce sustenance for each other in a spot that was once just dust, wreckage of the SS *Imo* and the SS *Mont-Blanc* and the many homes and lives lost.

When I was younger, I was quite enticed by the neighbourhood known as the Hydrostone, and not just because it was the absolute best place to go trick-or-treating. Even as a young kid, I used the shared green public space in between the boulevards for games of soccer, football, and to gather with friends and gossip. But unknown to me at the time, the Hydrostone, built following the Halifax Explosion, was an ingenious model of housing for working-class families that prioritized structural integrity and community. With its distinct row houses, with their cement faces on parallel streets, tall trees, and green spaces, the Hydrostone was recognized in 2011 as the second-greatest neighbourhood in Canada.

It's hard to believe that the Hydrostone wasn't designed or built yesterday with our most modern technology and our newest urban planning practices. I think what we can take away from this is that, when rebuilding, the designers learned from the past. They learned from the disaster to prioritize community and to build homes that were more resistant to fire. We now have to look at what we know is a threat to the integrity and history of our communities and our values; we need to say no to development that prioritizes profit over community, liveability, and the environment. If Haligonians, with the help of neighbouring provinces and the US, could make those things a priority in the years following the explosion, I believe that we can make our communities and our environment a priority today. We need to learn from our history. We need to respect what our ancestors learned from the disasters they faced, so that we can raise families here and continue to give back to our communities.

—

The poignant and unique contributions from Catherine Martin, Juanita Peters, and Paige Farah are reminders that the narratives and accounts of the explosion remain unfinished, as many stories are still undiscovered and waiting to be shared. The explosion continues to reverberate through family histories, neighbourhoods, and communities, as these moving accounts reveal.

NOTES

1 Support for "Towards Explosion 2017: Perspectives on the Centenary of the Halifax Explosion" was provided through the SSHRC Connection Program, and project partners Narratives in Space+Time Society, NSCAD University, Dalhousie Art Gallery, Maritime Museum of the Atlantic, Canadian Science and Technology Museum, Wonder'neath Art Society, and Dalhousie School of Architecture.

"Walking the Debris Field": Narratives for Peace

Robert Bean and Angela Henderson

WALKING AND DÉRIVE

Walking has become a measure of ideal community design and a tool in public policy. With the introduction of the term *walkability*, pedestrian experience has become a way of assessing the quality of urban life and establishing everything from real estate values to plans and policies for urban design and development.

In 2012, Narratives in Space+Time Society (NiS+TS), consisting of Robert Bean, Brian Lilley, Barbara Lounder, and Mary Elizabeth Luka, began informally with a series of exploratory walks with friends and colleagues within the urban geography of Kjipuktuk (Halifax Harbour). The walks were influenced by Barbara Lounder's solo *Ghost Walk* from the Bedford Basin to the Sexton Campus of Dalhousie University on December 6, 2011, to commemorate the Halifax Explosion and the École Polytechnique massacre (December 6, 1989). The group's early walks were in urban areas that were not always convenient or aesthetically open to taking a stroll; forgotten and overlooked spaces as well as liminal sites with boundaries attracted the group's curiosity, with the walking frequently mediated by GPS systems and mobile media apps that were then becoming more accessible.

These preliminary explorations approached the act of walking as a mediation between active experience and the creation of knowledge, stories, and ideas. This thinking is informed by psychogeography, the study of the emotional, psychological, and political meanings of urban space to create alternative understandings of urban existence. Psychogeography, introduced by Guy Debord and the Letterist

International in 1953, uses acts of walking known as dérives (or drifts). Debord defines dérive as "a mode of experimental behavior linked to the conditions of urban society: a technique of transient passage through varied ambiances" (Knabb 1981, 45). More simply put, a dérive is an unplanned journey through a landscape, usually urban, where the surrounding architecture and geography subconsciously direct the walk with the goal of encountering an entirely new and authentic experience.

During one dérive, the group entered Shannon Park, an abandoned military housing complex in the north end of Dartmouth. At the time, there was a sense of apprehension and exhilaration about crawling through a fence with signs warning trespassers of prosecution. The site was in ruin: fields of weeds cluttered with rusted clotheslines, swing sets, and an extraordinary gallery of unauthorized urban graffiti. Most of the windows in the buildings had been smashed, and we became aware that this may not be the safest place to explore. At the same time, it was clear that another community had made its presence visible—dog walkers, grazing deer, graffiti artists, and staff from the Bedford Institute of Oceanography who used the site for walks and lunch breaks. After wandering through the abandoned streets, we made our way to the shoreline to view Halifax from the Dartmouth side of the Narrows (Kepe'k). A renewed sense of awareness and astonishment occurred as we surveyed the site of the Halifax Explosion from close proximity. This was the defining moment for a four-year walking and public art project by NiS+TS titled "Walking the Debris Field: Public Geographies of the Halifax Explosion."

"WALKING THE DEBRIS FIELD"

The NiS+TS project defined the debris field as the contemporary urban geography of Halifax and Dartmouth influenced by the Halifax Explosion and its history. The main locations that comprise the debris field include ground zero (Pier 6), Mulgrave Park, the neighbourhood of Richmond, the Hydrostone, Fort Needham Park, Africville,

Admiralty House Naval Museum, the Irving Halifax Shipyard, the Halifax Graving Dock, Her Majesty's Canadian Dockyard, the historic Exhibition Grounds once located at Robie, Almon, and Young streets, Turtle Grove (Kepe'kek), Tufts Cove, and Shannon Park.

The explosion is held in the public imagination as a traumatic and perhaps inevitable tragedy. It functions within disaster tourism as an event to be commemorated, but not scrutinized or critiqued. With this in mind, we did not want the public walks to be "tours" reiterating an official history. Rather, we created public art events in the form of walking that emphasized present experience. We frequently reminded participants and collaborators that "today we will make history." The historical moment of the Halifax Explosion is distant, while the experience of walking its debris field is immediate. The eighteenth- and nineteenth-century Halifax street grid that existed at the time of the explosion is buried under a web of infrastructure, even as we cross its verges today.

The NiS+TS walking projects adopted a variety of formats. Frequently, we conducted informal research walks to learn more about the social and urban geography of the debris field. On many occasions, we invited others to contribute to these excursions. During the four years leading up to the 2017 centenary, we hosted five public walking events as well as a centenary procession for December 6, 2017. In addition, we arranged two boat trips on the harbour to retrace the fateful voyage of the SS *Mont-Blanc*, the French munitions ship that exploded on the morning of December 6, 1917. We also assisted with several commemoration events organized by Elders and members of the local Mi'kmaw community at the ancestral site of their descendants.

The many collaborators who participated and contributed their voices and perceptions to an inclusive and alternative remembrance of the explosion were a significant attribute of the public walks. Participants included actors, musicians, historians, scientists, storytellers, visual artists, designers, and architects, as well as community leaders from Africville, Mulgrave Park, and Millbrook First Nation.

Many of the collaborations were improvised, offering creative choices to contributors and presenters.

While histories can appear to be static narratives, the fact is that we all make and remake history every day through our own experiences and the stories we tell. One problem that we discovered through the debris field project was how the public narratives that dominated the history of the Halifax Explosion were not inclusive, nor did they acknowledge the range of the contemporary social and urban geography of the explosion. For instance, one of the best locations from which to view the geography of the harbour in relation to ground zero, the former location of Pier 6 where the explosion occurred, is in the neighbourhood of Mulgrave Park. Retaining the location name that predates the explosion of 1917, Mulgrave Park is a housing development built in 1964 to relocate a diverse neighbourhood from downtown Halifax that was on the site of the Cogswell Interchange. Even though Mulgrave Park is in the heart of Richmond, the neighbourhood that was obliterated by the Halifax Explosion, there is virtually nothing (markers, plaques, etc.) that identifies today's Mulgrave Park with the history of the explosion.

Another example of historical absence is the location of ground zero (Pier 6). Based on mapping analysis and urban morphology conducted by NiS+TS and James Boxall at the GIS Centre at Dalhousie University, the former location of Pier 6 is most probably inside the large white Ultra Hall of the Halifax Shipyard where the new Arctic patrol ships designed to monitor Canada's northern territories are currently being assembled by Irving Shipbuilding. The new frigates for Canada's combatant fleet will also be manufactured at the Irving Halifax Shipyard. In this context, the shipyard, already haunted by the militarism of previous wars, is optimistically preparing for another potential disaster due to the rapid depletion of ice in the Arctic region today.[1]

Descending from Fort Needham Memorial Park, the setting of the recently renovated Halifax Explosion Memorial Bell Tower, down

Richmond Street to the Ultra Hall of the shipyard, there are no visible markers or commemorations of the explosion. In short, the closer you get to ground zero, the more invisible the explosion becomes. Indeed, it is common for Haligonians and visitors to mistake the Hydrostone neighbourhood where the relief housing was built as the site of the explosion. Even though the Hydrostone neighbourhood is a kilometre away from ground zero, the marking of the relief housing as a national historic site encourages the perception that the explosion took place there rather than at the current site of the Halifax Shipyard.

Heading down Richmond Street toward the Halifax Shipyard and site of Pier 6, NiS+TS staged a collaborative presentation about the Acadia Sugar Refinery that was also located on the current site of the shipyard and destroyed in the explosion. The refinery processed sugar from Richmond, Virginia, which is how the neighbourhood got its name, a name that is a reminder of the history of slavery in the sugar industry. The proximity of the Richmond neighbourhood to the former site of Africville, one of the earliest settlements of African Nova Scotians, is a rarely acknowledged history that perpetuates additional misperceptions about the contemporary debris field.

NiS+TS commissioned local architect Anton Christiansen to create a scale model of the sugar refinery using laser-cut box board filled with sugar cubes. During the group's inaugural public walk on December 6, 2014, this model was set on fire and allowed to burn to ashes. The smell of caramelizing sugar completed the multi-sensorial moment. Acting as a counter-monument, the burning model created a memory of the present, which revealed the significance of the location and how it is possible to create ephemeral commemorative events that introduce inclusive narratives. Similar to the act of walking itself, this temporary practice of counter-memorial was inherent to all NiS+TS walks and projects that followed.

MONUMENTS AND COUNTER-MONUMENTS

Traditionally, monuments are historical markers of a nation's victories and calamities, intended to determine collective memory by immortalizing persons or events of extraordinary significance. Constructed under the auspices of government authorities, monuments reinstate dominant political narratives. Within our public spaces, monuments actively affirm privilege while confirming disparity, silently re-enforcing the authority of the ruler over the ruled. In contrast, counter-monuments reject authoritarianism, insisting on cognitive dissonance and diversion to question assumptions that histories, as they are written, are impartial in their account. Multiple voices, perspectives, and interpretations, enacted in the time-space event of walking, are encouraged by NiS+TS, whereby the production of a new space forms from alternative understandings of historical events.

Following the counter-memorial to the sugar refinery in 2014, NiS+TS commissioned visual artist Angela Henderson to produce four additional board models that were burned during public walks between 2015 and 2018. Henderson also created artistic keepsakes that were given to those who participated, and a set of four counter-monument models, based on the models that were burned, was exhibited at the Chase Gallery of the Nova Scotia Archives in December 2017, in conjunction with the NiS+TS Archive Exhibition.

Drawing on fragmented documentation of the former buildings (postage stamps, archival photos, etc.), Henderson created composite architectural models of the four civic buildings lost in the explosion: the aforementioned sugar refinery, a schoolhouse, a cotton mill, and a train house. Following a presentation on the site of the former buildings, the models were burned, only ashes remaining in the wake of these poignant spectacles. The transitory nature of these models as counter-monuments spoke to a nuance and subtlety in works of public commemoration. Participants in these acts of commemoration only have the memory of these structures being erased through the spectacle of a re-enacted "explosion" and the disappearance of the original buildings.

In 2018, the last burning model was added to the series, a mega-industrial boatbuilding facility situated geographically at ground zero within the sightline of a sanctioned monument to the original catastrophe, the Halifax Explosion Memorial Bell Tower in Fort Needham Memorial Park. The site-specific performance took place against the backdrop of the massive Ultra Hall of the Irving Halifax Shipyard, where the model was burned during the final public event. The model was constructed from a series of laser-cut steel trusses; the model's paperboard cladding, when burned away, revealed the structure's steel skeleton. Through the flames, the charred metal structure of the shipyard emerged, followed by the ceramic forms of colliding ships. The ceramic ships, created by Estonian artist Juss Heinsalu, underwent an unusual firing process, by which the porous forms were buried in hot coals. This second wave of heat exposed the ships to the ashes of the incinerated model and imprinted traces of carbon on the ships in the aftermath of the flames.

Following these counter-monuments of burning models, questions remained on how to maintain an ephemeral approach to memorialization while still presenting the work in an archival exhibition that is intended to exist in perpetuity. To achieve this, Henderson created a speculative work, structurally ephemeral through an abstraction of site and architecture. Adhering to principles similar to minimalist sculpture, the destroyed structures were memorialized with materials that were in direct contrast to the previous work created for NiS+TS. The four models were assembled from multiple striations of clear Perspex, rendering an invisible structure embedded within a cast concrete landscape. By reducing the scale of these buildings to miniature, a speculative form stands in as a memory of these spaces; the work is permanent and accessible, yet it crosses multiple timelines within Halifax's contemporary urban North End. As scaled miniatures with discreet reference to the original structures, these works act as

Figure 5. Burning model, Irving Halifax Shipyard, "Walking the Debris Field: Centenary Procession," December 3, 2017. (NARRATIVES IN SPACE+TIME SOCIETY)

Figure 6. Architectural models by Angela Henderson with images of site-specific burnings by Robert Bean. Debris Field Archives Exhibition *at the Chase Gallery, NS Archives, Halifax, December 2017.* (NARRATIVES IN SPACE+TIME SOCIETY)

counter-monuments in that they invite viewers to form their own subjective interpretations and embrace diverse narratives that critically engage with ideas of public memorialization and memory.

NOTES

1 The building of Arctic patrol ships and frigates in an area with a depressed economy demonstrates the inherent conflict between militarization, climate change, and an inadequate environmental policy. Funded by the Department of National Defence, only a very small percentage of the overall shipbuilding portion of the budget supports research projects addressing the climate crisis, while many of the allotments are directed toward expanding commercialization and economic interests in the Arctic region (Irving Shipbuilding Inc. 2016). The most recent report from the International Panel on Climate Change (2022) indicates that the risks and consequences of climate change in the polar regions are profound and demand an urgent and accelerated response. A primary area of concern is the impact on Arctic Indigenous Peoples.

Chapter 7

Peace Activism

Introduction

Maya Eichler

Canadians tend to remember their military heroes, not their military critics (Teigrob 2016). This seems to be equally true for subpopulations of the Canadian collective such as Nova Scotians. As noted earlier, a recounting of Nova Scotia's history is usually a recounting of its military history and heroes. But the province has a rich and long history of peace advocacy. Peace activism in Nova Scotia has taken many forms, with local, national, and global areas of focus. It has involved diverse actors—women and men, veterans and civilians, activists and scholars. Remembering this part of Nova Scotia's history is important. This chapter describes some of this history, illuminating the importance of including peace activism in the stories we tell about our province.

Halifax historian Sharon MacDonald unearthed one such story—that of Mary Russell Chesley (1847–1923) of Lunenburg. During the First World War, Chesley was an energetic leader in the Woman's Christian Temperance Union (WCTU) as well as a suffragist and peace advocate. At a 1915 union meeting, she exclaimed, "We of the little Nova Scotia WCTU may not have a part in peace conferences but let us not forget that we are all followers of the Prince of Peace.... And let us try to remember that it is not by the slaughter of Germans or Austrians war will be ended, but by the dethronement of military ideals—whether they be German, Russian, French or British" (McDonald 2010, 53). Chesley maintained pacifist principles throughout the war and made it clear that she did not accept the vote as "payment" for war work. She founded the first Canadian chapter of the Women's

International League for Peace and Freedom—a leading international feminist peace organization that is still active today, though it no longer has a presence in Nova Scotia. Pacifist principles were ingrained in Chesley's family, leading her daughter Polly to India to work with Mahatma Gandhi decades later (McDonald 2010).

While Chesley was an early advocate for peace, much of Nova Scotia's most impactful peace activism took place during the Cold War years. It was then that the Thinkers Lodge belonging to Cyrus Eaton in Pugwash became a prominent site for international peace efforts. Spurred by the release of the Russell–Einstein Manifesto in 1955, which warned about the dangers of war in the nuclear age, Eaton invited the signatories and others to Pugwash in 1957. The meeting led Joseph Rotblat and Bertrand Russell to found what came to be known as the Pugwash Conferences on Science and World Affairs. Ever since, the Pugwash Conferences have brought together scientists and public figures in different locations around the globe to work toward "a world free of nuclear weapons and other weapons of mass destruction." The Pugwash movement is informed by the ethos of "dialogue across divides" (Pugwash Conferences, n.d.). During the Cold War, the Pugwash Conferences facilitated communication between the Soviet Union and the US, paving the road for the signing of key international treaties such as the nuclear test ban and non-proliferation treaties. In 1995, Rotblat and the Pugwash Conferences on Science and World Affairs jointly won the Nobel Peace Prize "for their efforts to diminish the part played by nuclear arms in international politics and, in the longer run, to eliminate such arms" (The Nobel Peace Prize 1995). Pugwash groups are active globally to this day, continuing their work toward nuclear disarmament and eventual abolition.

During the Cold War, Nova Scotia also became a prominent site for women's peace activism. The Canadian Voice of Women for Peace (also known as the Voice of Women) was founded in 1960. Its premise at that time was that women's maternal role gave them a special responsibility to preserve life and end violence. The Voice of Women emphasized the importance of studying and preparing for peace rather than war and, not unlike the Pugwash movement, of working across the East–West divide. In Nova Scotia, key activists in the movement included Muriel Duckworth and Betty Peterson, who worked alongside activists such as Ursula Franklin and Marion Kerans in other parts of Canada (Brookfield 2012; Early 2005). This chapter includes reflections on the past and present of the Voice of Women. In "Nova Scotia Voice of Women for Peace: From Cold War Origins to a Hot Planet," kathrin winkler, a current member of Nova Scotia Voice of Women (NSVOW), writes on the origins and continued relevance of this historic feminist peace group at the national and provincial levels. She outlines NSVOW's early activism and their current educational campaigns. Making specific connections between the military-industrial complex and the current climate crisis, winkler asserts that feminist peace work is more necessary now than ever.

In the 1960s, peace activism in Nova Scotia was further fueled by Canadian veterans who took up the cause of peace and by the arrival of US Vietnam War resisters, as highlighted by two stories in this chapter. In "Giff Gifford: From Second World War Bomber to Veteran Against Nuclear Arms," Brian Gifford tells the story of his father, from his upbringing and the beginning of his military career to his work as a dedicated peace activist campaigning internationally for denuclearization. Drawing largely from a family archive, Gifford details his father's valuable contributions to the work of Veterans Against Nuclear Arms (VANA) and reflects on a life of peace activism shaped by military service. VANA's veterans used their experience of war to stress the need for peace. The organization was active for thirty-two years, and its last remaining chapter closed in 2014. Unlike the US, Canada no longer has a veteran peace movement.

The Cold War brought many Vietnam War resisters, draft evaders, and deserters from the US to Canada, including to Nova Scotia. It is estimated that as many as forty thousand US citizens settled in

Canada as a result of their opposition to the war. "Yes to Canada! No to War!" is the story of Roger Davies, a US Vietnam War resister who lives in Nova Scotia. But it is more than the story of a draft resister coming to Canada. In his reflection, Davies tells of how he found a community after his arrival in Canada through his involvement in social causes such as Men for Change and the resettlement of refugees. He also problematizes the connections between militarism and masculinity and considers his grandson's decision to join the Canadian Armed Forces.

Just as Davies continues his peace activism today, so do many other Nova Scotians. More recent efforts include the Halifax Peace Coalition which formed in the lead-up to the 2003 US invasion of Iraq. Active from 2003 to 2014 in the context of the post-9/11 global war on terror, this coalition of faith-based, social justice, labour, and peace groups engaged in peace activities such as vigils, letter-writing campaigns, and awareness raising. Local peace activists also lobbied for Halifax to join Mayors for Peace—a goal achieved in 2014 (Bousquet 2014). This Japanese-based peace initiative brings together thousands of cities globally working toward nuclear abolition. In 2020, at the urging of local peace groups such as NSVOW, Halifax Regional Council passed a motion in support of an international cities-based campaign to abolish nuclear weapons. While this was largely a symbolic step, such activities keep issues of peace on the agenda locally. Another key actor in the local peace movement has been the Halifax anti-war group No Harbour for War, which has been calling for a nuclear-free port. The group has also been organizing annual protests against the Halifax Security Forum, an international organization that brings together politicians, defence experts, defence industry representatives, and representatives from international governmental and non-governmental organizations to discuss security challenges and strategic cooperation. Protesting against the Halifax Security Forum has become a key annual activity for the local peace community, which sees the event as reinforcing militarization and bolstering the defence industry. We end this chapter with a spoken word poem performed by Halifax's former Poet Laureate El Jones during the 2016 demonstration against the Halifax Security Forum. Her poem "We Built This City" names the violent military and colonial history of Halifax and challenges how this history is perpetuated through events such as the Halifax Security Forum.

The stories told in this chapter are usually overshadowed by the dominant military narrative of Nova Scotia, but they are equally a part of the province's history. The contributors highlight the diversity of the peace movement in the past and present through the stories of the veteran peace movement, the women's peace movement, US war resisters coming to Canada, and ongoing peace protests in Halifax today. They offer a glimpse into some of the many ways in which Nova Scotians have worked to challenge militarization and bring us closer to peace.

Nova Scotia Voice of Women for Peace: From Cold War Origins to a Hot Planet

kathrin winkler

War is the greatest destroyer of human life, the greatest polluter, the greatest creator of refugees, the greatest cause of starvation and illness. We all have to care—not just for our own little circle, but for the universe.
(Muriel Duckworth, quoted in Senate of Canada 2009, 1377)

On June 14, 2019, Canada declared a national climate emergency. Now more than ever, it is crucial for each one of us to reflect on how this declaration affects our perspective on peace and war. There is a direct link between the business of war and environmental devastation, but that link is often hidden by the mythologies of nationalism and capitalism. Peace activism is driven by the hope of addressing the root causes of violence and moving beyond them.

Canadian Voice of Women for Peace (VOW) is the oldest feminist peace organization in Canada. The determination to speak out against militarism comes from the strength of the women who came before us and whose memory we carry forward. In February 2018, one of the great Nova Scotian peace women, Betty Peterson, passed away at the age of one hundred. Peterson was known for her motto, "Keep on keepin' on," and for her perseverance that inspired the Nova Scotia chapter of Voice of Women for Peace (NSVOW). Peterson and founding member Muriel Duckworth were resilient and prominent feminist leaders advocating tirelessly for peace initiatives and social reform. Members still active today speak of drinking tea with Duckworth and bolstering their mutual dedication. Long-standing steering committee members such as Sandy Greenburg and Linda Christiansen-Ruffman often remind newer members of Duckworth's words, that "war is stupid" and that there are no "good" wars (Nova Scotia Advisory Council on the Status of Women 2014, 38).

VOW was founded in Toronto in 1960, and Duckworth became involved immediately, forming a Halifax chapter within months. In 1967, she went on to become the national president of VOW. Twenty women attended the first NSVOW meeting in her living room. Global issues such as nuclear testing in Atlantic waters and nuclear dumps off the coast of Yarmouth threatened the shores of Nova Scotia. Aware of the dangers of radioactive fallout, VOW members presented a brief to the Canadian government, and they participated in and supported research by collecting thousands of baby teeth to test for the presence of strontium-90. This campaign created public awareness of the dangers of nuclear radioactivity. It also pointed clearly to the link between the military-industrial complex and environmental degradation. The environmental destruction caused by the military during the Vietnam War led VOW to investigate the dangers of oil and gas development in the Canadian north and its impact on Indigenous communities.

Membership in the national organization climbed to six thousand in the 1970s. Now, almost half a century later, active membership in NSVOW is less than one hundred. Some could say that the group is not a strong voice for justice and peace anymore. Peace actions are carried out by a dwindling group of dedicated participants. And although only a few women meet monthly in members' living rooms, my own view is that we do what we can, where we can, and that everything counts. We know more work is needed in our outreach to the next generation. How to be more effective at intergenerational mentoring is one of our greatest challenges. As a non-governmental organization, we offer young people the chance to attend the annual session of the UN Commission on the Status of Women in New York, and this annual trip to New York continues to draw enthusiastic participants.

NSVOW continues to initiate community events to call attention to militarism and its folly. The dominant narrative is that military history *is* the story of the nation. As peace activists, we ask ourselves, "How can we project a different narrative?" One way is through participation in Nocturne. Held annually, the Nocturne festival is an evening of popular art throughout Halifax and Dartmouth that includes displays by individual artists and community groups. Participating in the event is a way for NSVOW to engage the public with peace activism through re-envisioning ourselves and our history. Our participation in 2017 engaged the public in rethinking how weapons are displayed and encouraged new stories about public encounters with the military presence in Halifax.

Cannons are displayed throughout Halifax. The purpose of a cannon is as a weapon—to maim, kill, and destroy. For Nocturne in 2017, a cannon was covered with white poppies that included expressions of hope for peace written by members of the public. In 2018, our installation was a continuous public reading of the Truth and Reconciliation Commission's report in front of the empty pedestal where the statue of Edward Cornwallis once stood. We believe that healing ourselves and our earth is not possible in a state of denial of the genocide of our missing and murdered sisters, the residential school system, and the ongoing injustices toward Indigenous Peoples.

Connecting the dots between military spending and environmental degradation is another way we hope to amplify the call to justice. Every spring, we highlight the Global Campaign on Military Spending in front of the Halifax Central Library by engaging citizens in an interactive exercise that highlights how much of taxpayers' money goes into the defence coffers. Our campaign banner emphasizes our peace priority: Demilitarize. Decarbonize. We set up a table with jars labelled Women and Children, Health, Education, The Arts, Environment, and Military/Defence. Passersby are given a dollar to represent their tax dollars and are invited to place the coin in the jar where they would like their money spent. Military spending is consistently chosen least of all. Yet, Canada spends nearly twenty times more on national defence than it spends on the environment and climate change or Indigenous and Northern Affairs (Wilt 2017). Most of our participants would re-allocate those funds to health care, environmental protection, or the needs of women and children.

Another facet of our peace activism is our anti-nuclear advocacy. NSVOW's anti-nuclear advocacy encourages officials to sign the 2017 UN Treaty on the Prohibition of Nuclear Weapons. This international agreement, brought to life through the International Campaign to Abolish Nuclear Weapons, prohibits weapons of mass destruction and establishes a clear pathway to their elimination. Canada did not participate in the negotiation of the UN Treaty on the Prohibition of Nuclear Weapons and voted against the UN General Assembly resolution in 2016 that established the mandate for nations to negotiate the treaty. Canada claims that US nuclear weapons are essential for its security. NSVOW sent a letter to Halifax's mayor requesting that members of council support the UN treaty publicly; after all, our city belongs to Mayors for Peace. As stated on the Mayors for Peace website, "On June 24, 1982,...then Mayor Takeshi Araki of Hiroshima called for cities throughout the world to transcend national borders and join in solidarity to work together to press for nuclear abolition." In 2020, NSVOW started a petition calling on Mayor Savage and the Halifax Regional Municipality to support the International Campaign to Abolish Nuclear Weapons Cities Appeal ("A call for HRM to join the ICAN CITY APPEAL") that was signed by over nine hundred citizens. Supporting this campaign is a commitment to encourage governments around the world to sign and ratify the UN Treaty on the Prohibition of Nuclear Weapons. This action served as a reminder for all Nova Scotians that cities are the main targets of nuclear weapons and municipalities have a special responsibility to their constituents to speak out against any role for nuclear weapons in national security doctrines. Despite the opposition of five councillors, the motion introduced by Councillor Richard Zurawski passed with the support of Mayor Mike Savage and the rest of council (Devet 2020).

The invisible and untold numbers of civilian casualties caused by war, and particularly the vulnerability of women and children, can be overlooked in traditional patriotic views of war. NSVOW members wear white poppies year-round as a visual reminder of the true cost of war, though they often also wear a red poppy beside the white one for Remembrance Day. Members wear the white poppy as a "pledge to peace that war must not happen again" (Peace Pledge Union, n.d.), and distribute them for free in November. This campaign is central to our group as we firmly believe that peace is the path to peace.

White poppies, anti-nuclear actions, and demilitarization are some of our national campaigns, but closest to my heart has been NSVOW's participation in the Wabanaki Water Walk 2019, which recognized the sacred role of water in Indigenous cultures in a world that commercializes, exploits, and poisons waterways. Through the Wabanaki Water Walk 2019, we supported the water protectors of the Stop Alton Gas campaign. The earth provides for all our needs, but not for the greed that has so many life forms teetering on the edge of extinction. The Alton Gas company had planned to create large underground salt caves near Stewiacke to store high-pressure natural gas, flushing millions of litres of brine into the Shubenacadie River in the process and adding to ongoing environmental devastation. The campaign against this was led by Mi'kmaw grandmothers and rights holders, and it ensured the safety of everyone in the watershed.

Let me end with the voice of one of our VOW activists. Tamara Lorincz, one of Canada's foremost experts on the link between the military and greenhouse gas emissions, spells it out clearly: "Peace has got to be fundamental to the environmental movement. If it is not, we will not succeed" (Olds and Rutgers 2018, 3).

Giff Gifford: From Second World War Bomber to Veteran Against Nuclear Arms

Brian Gifford

C. G. "Giff" Gifford stood in front of a crowd in the Halifax Parade Square, snow falling gently on his tan wool winter coat. His voice and demeanour matched the crisp clarity of the air: "Any armed conflict can escalate to a nuclear war which would devastate humankind and the earth that sustains us. Armed conflict is obsolete."[1]

This was in the 1990s, one of many times Giff stood in front of a crowd speaking a truth that moved him deeply—a truth derived from his own experience in the Second World War. He explained the connection to the assembled demonstrators: "I bombed Dresden in 1945. Twelve hundred airplanes with eight thousand to nine thousand crew slaughtered a hundred thousand innocent residents and refugees."[2] Giff hesitated as tears welled up. "A few weeks later, one airplane with twelve crew members bombed Hiroshima, killing twice as many people, mostly civilians, half of them over a long drawn-out agony. The nuclear age challenges all of us to stop the insanity." His words moved the demonstrators. He spoke for Veterans Against Nuclear Arms (VANA), which was part of a broader peace movement that included many in Nova Scotia, across Canada, and around the world. The group started in response to the nuclear arms race in the 1980s and continued as the Gulf War flared in the early 1990s.

GIFF'S BACKSTORY

But let us go back to 1941, when Giff was twenty-three years old and his theology studies were interrupted by his enlistment in the Royal

Canadian Air Force (RAF). In May 1944, he became a navigator for a crew in the Pathfinder Force of the United Kingdom's Royal Air Force Bomber Command. Pathfinder aircraft went ahead of the bombers to mark their targets with flares. He flew forty-nine missions, earning the Distinguished Flying Cross.

In "Pathfinder," a chapter in the 1992 book *This Was My War*, Giff writes,

> *Only much later did I question whether the bombing of cities was a moral activity and militarily effective. I learned that the Bishop of Chichester had questioned the bombing policy in 1943 in the British House of Lords and that Sir Archibald Sinclair, Secretary for Air in the British Cabinet, had lied in saying only military targets were being attacked.... I also learned that the RAF and especially a huge American Strategic Bombing Survey had shown that the bombing did not significantly reduce German war production.... Far from destroying the morale of the German people, the bombing stiffened their backs and their determination to fight on. So I grieve for the 45,000 allied aircrew, including my friends, who were lost in a useless policy, and for the hundreds of thousands of innocent German civilians who were also lost.* (145)

After the war, Giff changed course and became a social worker. Inspired by Albert Schweitzer, he joined the movement that led a successful campaign to stop above-ground nuclear tests in the late 1950s. In 1963, the Liberal Party under the leadership of Lester B. Pearson allowed nuclear weapons to be placed on American Bomarc missiles stationed in Canada. This decision disgusted Giff and led him to become a lifelong member of the New Democratic Party. He came close to winning a federal seat in Montreal's Notre-Dame-de-Grâce riding in the 1960s and later helped Alexa McDonough build the party in Nova Scotia. It was his career in social work that brought him to Nova Scotia in 1975 when he became the director of Dalhousie University's Maritime School of Social Work. As he neared retirement in 1982, he co-founded Veterans for Multilateral Nuclear

Disarmament (later renamed to VANA) with Kell Antoft and became its first national chair.

NUCLEAR BUILDUP

In the early 1980s, the US had over twenty thousand nuclear weapons; its arch-enemy in the Cold War, the Soviet Union, had over thirty thousand. The weapons buildup was justified by the doctrine of mutually assured destruction. Nuclear weapons of various types were capable of destroying human civilization and the living surface of the earth many times over. It was a particularly dangerous time as the US under President Ronald Reagan greatly expanded its military budget and launched a new destabilizing Strategic Defence Initiative, dubbed "Star Wars," an impractical and costly attempt to create a system to intercept and destroy thousands of incoming missiles during an attack. "Star Wars" was meant to undermine the doctrine and ensure that the US would survive a Soviet nuclear attack.

The most dangerous changes in the late 1970s and early 1980s were the placement of Soviet SS-20 missiles and American Gryphon cruise missiles and Pershing IIs in Europe; all were nuclear-armed. The cruise missiles could reach the Soviet Union in under an hour, evading radar along the way. The SS-20s could reach Germany, and the Pershing IIs could reach Moscow in less than ten minutes. Leaders on both sides had about five minutes to decide if a perceived attack was real or a false alarm and whether to launch a strike in retaliation. Submarines roamed the oceans, ready to launch Tomahawk nuclear missiles at any part of the globe with very little warning. Meanwhile Reagan called the Soviet Union the "Evil Empire," creating fear in the Soviet Union that their Second World War experience of being invaded by Germany would be repeated.

The peace movement grew to huge proportions in response to these ominous threats. A 1982 demonstration in New York City, home of the United Nations, involved almost one million people, and similar numbers marched in West Germany where many of the new weapons were deployed or were aimed. VANA and demonstrations in Halifax were part of this massive international movement. VANA warned of the dangers of accidental nuclear war by raising awareness of the many real accidents and miscalculations in the Second World War, which led to unnecessary casualties on both sides. The organization argued that such accidents and errors in judgment are bound to happen in war but warned that, in the nuclear age, they could be profoundly disastrous. Remarkably, a 2018 book *1983: The World at the Brink* chillingly validates this warning by describing a period when American aggression and malfunctioning Soviet warning systems brought the world to within minutes of Armageddon on a few occasions (Kastner 2018).

VANA ACTIVISM

In an interview for an article that appeared in *Atlantic Insight Magazine*, Giff said of his peace activism, "I've re-enlisted. We went to war because we felt our children's future was in danger. Now it's very much in danger and we've signed up again" (Mansour 1986). VANA attracted many retired armed service personnel from all branches of the Canadian military who were deeply concerned about the nuclear arms race and the potential for nuclear annihilation. Within a few years, VANA had as many as nine hundred members nationally in eleven branches, with particularly strong branches in Nova Scotia and British Columbia (Mills 1989, C14). The organization operated from 1982 to the mid-1990s, with Giff at its helm until his untimely death from a stroke in 1993. There was a sense of camaraderie in VANA that, in some ways, resembled the camaraderie of military units in wartime. While they were battling under gentler conditions, VANA members were united in their view that costly and dangerous preparations for nuclear war must end.

VANA prepared detailed booklets and briefs offering an alternative to war. As chair of VANA, Giff was usually the spokesperson. The apparent contradiction and novelty of veterans against war, combined with the compelling war stories and knowledgeable analysis, meant VANA was often well covered in the media, even though its perspective did not align with the mainstream consensus (Benjamin 1989,

19). Giff participated in peace marches and met with local community peace groups across the country, held press conferences in local Legions, presented briefs to the government, and worked with similar veteran groups in other countries.

VANA engaged with policy debates through its sister organization, the Defence Research and Education Centre. Its response to "Competitiveness and Security: Directions for Canada's International Relations," a 1985 Green Paper on Canada's international relations, was "Toward a World Without War: Next Steps in Canadian Defence Policy." This report presented a comprehensive alternative to the reliance on nuclear weapons to maintain a precarious, dangerous peace. Three Nova Scotia VANA members, Giff, Captain (Retired) Ray Creery, and Hugh Taylor, were the primary authors, with input from fifty other VANA members, twelve of whom were Nova Scotian. In their report, they advocated for a "negotiation and world law approach" to security to replace the dangerous, prevailing "permanent arms race approach." Their ideas included ending the arms race and reducing stockpiles through negotiated reductions and security guarantees for each side; supporting international instruments of co-operation, negotiation, and settlement of disputes such as the United Nations and the World Court; and shifting resources from war making to social and economic development that would help build the conditions of lasting peace (Defence Research and Education Centre 1987). They published two additional reports in the Towards a World Without War series in 1987–88, responding to the 1987 White Paper on defence policy.

When the USS *Atlanta,* an American nuclear-armed submarine capable of carrying twelve Tomahawk missiles, docked in Halifax Harbour in 1986, Giff protested in the local media and also joined public protests. He said, "I'm not surprised it is here. It is part of a very stupid policy. Each of the Tomahawks has 100 times the power of the Halifax Explosion of 1917. That's minus the radiation" (Hoare 1986). Halifax is only too aware of what such destructive power can mean.

On November 6, 1992, Giff presented a brief to the Senate during a hearing on the controversial National Film Board film *Death by Moonlight: Bomber Command,* which was shown on CBC as part of a series, *The Valour and the Horror*. The film examined Canadian and Allied participation in the Second World War bombing campaign under the leadership of Arthur Harris, the head of Britain's Bomber Command who was nicknamed "Bomber Harris." Giff supported the film's view that Canadian airmen were courageous, and agreed with its position that the purpose behind Harris's policy of civilian carpet-bombing was concealed during the war and led to mass deaths in Germany and among Allied air crews, as it achieved almost nothing. Other veteran groups loudly condemned the film, arguing that it denigrated the participation of Canadians and other air crews as well as the reputation of Air Marshall Harris. Giff's view was that we must learn from our mistakes in war by looking at the evidence. He argued that, by censoring critical views, we would betray the very principles we were fighting for. The film's potential impact was reduced due to its condemnation by the Senate's Subcommittee on Veterans Affairs in its January 1993 Senate report, also titled *The Valour and the Horror*.

INTERNATIONAL EFFORTS AND LOCAL ALLIES

Giff was the subject of *Return to Dresden,* a half-hour National Film Board film conceived and directed by Martin Duckworth, son of Nova Scotian peace activist Muriel Duckworth. The film follows Giff and his wife, Sylvia McDonald, as they travel to Dresden. The Dresden Opera House, which had been destroyed during the war, was re-opening on February 13, 1985, to commemorate the fortieth anniversary of the bombing. Giff met with peace activists and with ordinary citizens in a Dresden city square. The meeting became emotional as people angrily challenged Giff for his role in the useless slaughter of innocents. He responded by expressing his sorrow and regret and his desire to fight for peace. In the end, they thanked him for coming, and everyone mourned the tragedy of the attack and resolved to work toward a better future. Giff would be appalled to learn that the Dresden bombing has since become a rallying cry for today's German far right, which calls it a "holocaust," stirring hate instead of reconciliation and reflection.

Giff told Halifax's *Mail-Star* that "veterans' organizations of our kind are growing slowly around the world. I don't think it has ever happened before in history that you have career military people or civilians like me who were in uniform for four years devoting a lot of energy to trying to get the war machine destroyed" (Mills 1989, C14). Giff and other VANA members met with Soviet war veterans several times to discuss disarmament (Dunlop 1987). They also formed warm, mutually supportive relations with Veterans for Peace in the US, based in Maine. Their leader, Jerry Genesio, and Giff became good friends and attended each other's annual national meetings and shared information and analysis throughout the year. Jerry wrote of Giff, "He was a man who wore the Distinguished Flying Cross proudly, but found in it lessons rather than glory. Of all the leaders I have ever known, he was by far the kindest and gentlest" (Genesio 1993, 1).

Just as significant were VANA's allies at home. Canada had over a thousand peace groups in the early 1980s, and several were active in Nova Scotia (Pakula and Pancer 1985, 18). They were all part of the national Canadian Peace Alliance, an umbrella organization of anti-nuclear groups. Allies included the Voice of Women for Peace led by Nova Scotians Muriel Duckworth, Betty Peterson, and Sandy Greenberg. Muriel was a long-time family friend of Giff from the 1920s. They later became close personal friends and allies in the peace movement.

CONCLUSION

When VANA started, the world was a hair trigger away from nuclear annihilation, with two superpowers relying on weapons that could destroy European cities with millions of inhabitants with only ten minutes' warning. The 1987 Intermediate-Range Nuclear Forces (INF) Treaty was a major step back from the brink, and it occurred in part due to the massive peace movements of the 1980s, including

VANA. In 2019, the US announced that it would end the INF Treaty in response to alleged violations by Russia. This is insanity revisited. There is now a debate about autonomous weapons that can automatically respond to threats within seconds. This is another form of hair-trigger weaponry that threatens to undermine security in the nuclear age (Ayed 2019).

Gifford ended his chapter in *This Was My War* by writing, "Weapons are no longer simple tools of the military, they have become world destroyers and war itself must be abolished if civilization is to survive" (1992, 146). VANA members, including Giff, used their voices to work toward this goal, which surely must someday be achieved.

NOTES

1 This quote and the next one comparing Dresden to Hiroshima are statements Giff Gifford made many times, including at public demonstrations, as remembered by Brian Gifford, his son and the author of this piece. Similar statements appear in his writings and in media interviews and reports, for instance, in *This Was My War* (1992).

2 The number of deaths caused by the bombing of Dresden has been contentious. As reported by Kate Connolly in a 2008 online article for *The Guardian*, "While estimates for the numbers killed in the attacks on the city have fluctuated wildly between 35,000 and half a million over the past six decades, the historians commissioned by the city say the figure was considerably lower." Connolly, Kate. "Panel Rethinks Death Toll from Dresden Raids," *The Guardian*, October 3, 2008. theguardian.com/world/2008/oct/03/secondworldwar.germany.

Yes to Canada! No to War!

Roger Davies

May 10, 1968: One of the most important days of my life—right up there with being born, getting married, and the birth of our daughter. This was the day I was welcomed into Canada.

Up to that day, I had been living in the US. I had worked for years, along with millions of others, to end the horrific and, to my mind, immoral, war against Vietnam. When I was conscripted by legal force to fight in that war, it was clear to me that I could not—would not—betray my beliefs and my knowledge of the real reasons the US had attacked that small Asian country.

Along with thousands of others who were drafted, we made the choice to seek sanctuary and a new life in Canada. For me, it was relatively easy: my parents were supportive, I was fortunate to have had a good education, and I was ready to start anew in Canada. For many others, the choice was a hard one. If family had turned against them or if they were unsure about starting a new life here, the weeks and months ahead were a troubling time of dislocation and confusion. That was particularly true for people who had been soldiers and then refused to carry on soldiering.

On that day in May, I was well prepared to seek landed-immigrant status at the border crossing at Niagara Falls. I had been helped by the anti-draft network in the US that was in close contact with war-resister support in Canada. I had also been helped by Quakers, a faith group that became central to my faith practice and justice work later in my life.

In the early 1960s, the policy of the Canadian government was generally not supportive of US war resisters, but by 1968, it was possible to enter Canada and seek landed immigrant status without reference to one's draft status in the US. However, for deserters, the process remained difficult. No one knows for sure how many men and women came to Canada to escape the US war machine. It may have been fifty thousand. Statistics show a great spike of immigration to Canada from the US during those war years (Squires 2013).

In every major city and many small towns, Canadians were there to help—with finding places to live, finding jobs, and for moral and social support. Not all Canadians approved of us war resisters, but right across the country, many people thought the war was wrong and that we newcomers had made a courageous choice to refuse war (Squires 2013).

I will never forget the moment when the immigration officer shook my hand and said, "Welcome to Canada!" After all those years of struggle, I finally was welcomed into a country not at war, but trying to build a fair, diverse, and beautiful society. I was ready.

GIVING BACK TO CANADA

I was ready to try to give back to Canada what it had given to me. I wanted to participate in furthering equality and opportunity. I will never forget how fortunate I was to avoid being forced into the scourge of war and to have a fresh start in a country where I spoke the language, adapted easily to the culture and customs, and found, with little difficulty, meaningful work as a teacher. And I met a Canadian woman who became my wife.

Many of the roughly fifty thousand of us who came during the time of US conscription in the 1960s and 70s offered our talents to Canada. It was a significant boost to our new country. A federal government publication has described US Vietnam War resisters as "the largest, best-educated group this country had ever received" (Scott 2017).

In Halifax, I was able to get a job at an alternative school for early school leavers in a low-income area of the city. Later, I taught at a correctional centre, working with students on literacy skills and preparation for the high-school equivalency examination. For a dozen years, I worked in Halifax libraries, coordinating programs where community volunteers taught literacy skills and became learning partners for newly arrived immigrants and refugees. I found it such a fine way to build community.

After the killing of fourteen women at Polytechnique Montréal on December 6, 1989, a group of us in Halifax formed an initiative called Men for Change, aimed at educating youth on the issue of violence against women. We did hundreds of school workshops, and three of us wrote *The Healthy Relationships Curriculum*, an educational guide that sold over five thousand copies. Part of our work involved personal reflection and coming together in support groups to discuss how masculinity and beliefs and attitudes about gender helped or hindered our true selves and the society we lived in.

One part of our work was to help youth look at the link between gender stereotypes and the threat or actual use of violence. What was it about a hard masculinity that linked "being a man" with power and control? This issue was familiar to me: I had known the pressures of a militarized masculinity that equated "being a man" or "becoming a real man" with military service.

HOPE FOR THE FUTURE

I continue to be engaged in the community. My faith group, the Halifax Friends (Quaker) Meeting, works for social justice and strives to end needless suffering. Twice, we have sponsored refugees. The first time, we partnered with the Ethiopian Association of Nova Scotia to sponsor five Ethiopians who had been living in Kenya for years. The second sponsorship involved family reunification. I had been tutoring a new Canadian who had originally lived in Iraq. He and his wife had waited five years in a refugee camp in Syria (before the current war) for a country to accept them. I became friends with my student. His wife had family still in Bagdad—mom, sister, and brother. Could I help sponsor them, they asked. Again, through the Halifax Friends

Meeting, we were able to raise the money, help with the difficult paperwork, and work in conjunction with the Immigrant Services Association of Nova Scotia to bring the family members to Halifax. What a moment it was at the airport to be present at a reunion of family members who had been separated by war for ten years.

My grandson Keegan joined the Canadian Armed Forces as a reservist a few years ago. I give him my full support in the choice he has made. It is my hope that if he chooses a military career, he will not equate his being a man with a military role and will not be seen as a "real" man because he is in the military. I also strongly believe that the threat to Canada is not a potential military attack from another country, but rather the chaos and devastation that will be brought on—and, in fact, is already emerging—as a result of climate change. I hope the Canadian Armed Forces will further redefine their role so as to assist our country as floods, forest fires, and extreme severe weather become increasingly commonplace. If Keegan plays a role where such help is needed, I will be proud indeed.

In 2006, hundreds of US Vietnam War resisters gathered to talk about our lives since coming to Canada and to show support for war resisters who had recently arrived from the US after refusing to fight against Iraq. We heard speeches from Tom Hayden and George McGovern and listened to Country Joe and the Fish and Buffy Sainte-Marie. One of the outstanding moments of this event was when draft resisters, army dissenters, and veterans against the war in Vietnam met to exchange views, share beliefs, and find unity in the opposition we held against the US government war-makers. I heard people speak of how they never reconciled with family in the US, of how unquestioned beliefs about serving (what I would actually call "serving up one's life to the war machine"), duty, and patriotism trumped the love and care between their closest relatives. This is a tragic outcome of war not often discussed.

I have been ever mindful of the advantages I came with. I have tried to give back to Canada what it gave to me—a chance for a peaceful life in a great country. In that regard, I am like all newcomers who make a fresh start, striving to live a full life and give what we have to offer. The war resisters who refused to fight in Vietnam have added their skills, talents, and new ways of seeing to the Canadian experience. It is through that experience that I see the lives of all newcomers and have hoped to contribute what I have to offer.

To help with retaining this piece of Canadian history, I have recently published a book for youth that tells the story of the Americans who came to Canada because they refused to fight against Vietnam. There are other chapters in Canadian history that are often brought before the public, such as the wars that Canada has fought in, but those who resist war do not often get a place in history, in schools, or before the general public. The full picture of war, including the resistance to war, needs to be told and retold.

We Built This City

El Jones

We built this city on land we stole
Built this city
Built this city on land we stole

We built this city on Cornwallis and Britain
We built this city on colonialism
Built on Mi'kmaw land without permission
We built this city with ammunition
And now that it's risen we build it on prisons
We're building off mental disease and addictions
No industry left so we build on tourism
We're building a city of militarism
And off-record panels inside of the Westin
By Western officials with global ambitions
Built with taxpayers' dollars but deny us admission
New defense minister building with MacKay's traditions
We're building on rhetoric of change and transition
While behind closed doors it's the same old position
We build interventions and armed expeditions
We claim bombing campaigns are human rights propositions
We build up Trudeau, build with liberalism
Same military, same wars, just new government edition
We build while Indigenous women go missing
They build over bagpipes and lobster dinners
And then they go home and build nuclear winter

We built this city on capitalism
We build TPP and free-trade propositions
We build Walmarts to push out local competition
Build cheap Chinese goods in sweatshop conditions
We build the economy global acquisition
Send jobs offshore, unemployment decisions
Used up all the coal, cut the trees, overfishing
Build up the North End Africville demolition
We're building off poverty, armed forces enlistment
Can't get a job so you get a commission
Build up the shipyards to Irving's conditions
Ships start here we're building off wishing
Still building off Harper although we dismissed him
We're gentrifying the projects on that thirty billion
We're building this city on military missions
Building weapons and warships to use on brown children
We build off the blood of Afghans and Libyans
We're building with drone strikes on Yemen and Syrians
Collateral damage we take out civilians
We build global war over pipeline positions
We're building this city on carbon emissions
We're building a cycle of radicalism
We tortured Arar, extraordinary rendition
We built occupations just changed definitions
We helped to build ISIS, historical revision
We built Boko Haram to get oil from Nigerians
We build instability, build opposition
We destabilized the Mideast, societal demolition
We build arms trade with the Saudis, geopolitical divisions
We fight proxy wars by our allies' decision
We're one of the willing we build coalitions
With the US and NATO and Israeli politicians
We help to build settlements, walls and partitions

Build an open-air prison in Gaza for Palestinians
We're building in Africa, new colonial mission
Built a security state from the war on terrorism
Cyber surveillance built by government technicians
We built a spy network the new inquisition
We're building a world where we all are suspicious
We're building two classes of Canadian citizens
We build Islamophobia and hate crimes commission
We build off a racist immigration points system
We build off the Tattoo, military tradition
Lockheed Martin on campus helps bill our tuition
We say we're building new weapons to strike with precision
Building new drones with facial recognition
We're building an economy on death and attrition
We're building new treaties on nuclear fission
We build NGOs then we send in tacticians
We use foreign aid to build imperialism
We build occupations and call it assistance
We build cholera, refugee camps, malnutrition
We build piles of dead bodies and decomposition
We built a new world from 9/11 fruition
We're building this world off of war repetition
The theatre of war is an endless audition
We built Al-Qaeda, we're building militias
We build retaliation a cycle so vicious
New York, Beirut, Paris, Mali, and Garissa
Military strikes just further ignition
We build global war and there's no intermission
We're building ourselves out of human existence
And we're not bystanders we're not an omission
Because don't you hear that radio transmission
Don't you remember take it back to the beginning

We built this city
We built this city on land we stole
Built this city
We built this city on land we stole

Chapter 8

War and Art

Introduction

Reina Green and Jessica Lynn Wiebe

The topic of war and art, even when limited to the Nova Scotian context, is vast. There is a long history of such art, and there are, of course, many different types of artistic representation to consider—both two- and three-dimensional visual art forms in all their variations, as well as performance art, which adds a fourth dimension. Much of the art created in response to war has a commemorative or memorializing function, whether it is to celebrate a victory or to remember the dead and injured. That is certainly the case for public art associated with war.

While many works of art are housed in public and private art galleries and go unnoticed by most people in their daily lives, public art, often in the form of monuments and statues, is a different matter as it occupies public space. It is this form of war art that we particularly want to consider, both because of its relative permanence—monuments are normally built to withstand both time and weather—and their prevalence. Almost every community in Nova Scotia has some type of monument commemorating those who died in the First and Second World Wars.

The practice of erecting statues and building monuments to commemorate military battles was particularly popular in the nineteenth century and the first half of the twentieth century. Many of these statues are still present in our city and town squares, parks, and at the entrances to civic buildings. These artworks reflect past ideas about honour, patriotism, and self-sacrifice and emphasize a certain aspect of civic or national pride. They promote a particular version of history, most often from the "victor's" perspective. By presenting only one aspect of history, such commemorative statues and monuments present a simplified narrative that obstructs a deeper understanding of actual historic events.

These artworks were created as lasting memorials and to remind future generations of the past, but their very permanence may defeat their commemorative function. Fixed and unchangeable in nature, they can become invisible to those who pass by them every day (Young 1992, 94). They become part of the landscape with no memorializing value. Moreover, monuments with a traditional design, such as a war memorial in the shape of a commemorative cairn or a statue of the Unknown Soldier, fail to encourage observers to connect their own experiences with the event being memorialized. People are left with the impression that they have seen it all before (Reeves 2013). The passage of time can also affect interpretation of the events commemorated by an artwork. Artists have limited control over how their own generation interprets their work, and they have no control over how future generations will see it.

With the recognition that traditional monuments fail in their function as memorial aids, artists began moving away from creating such public artworks in the second half of the twentieth century. Instead, some have focused on creating counter-monuments. Scholar James E. Young first coined the term *counter-monument* in his examination of public art and memory. Artists and academics who are interested in how the public views monuments and their continuously changing meaning have followed his lead.

Young argues that traditional monuments present "petrified versions of history that bury the living" (1992, 295) and suggests instead that memorialization of an historic event is more likely with a counter-monument to encourage interaction and reflection. Counter-monuments draw people in to walk through them, to touch, to feel.

They also emphasize the passage of time—they may change in the course of a day due to the passage of the sun and shadow, or over the years with the growth and decay of plant matter. This emphasis on impermanence or temporal instability draws attention to the connection between time and memory and challenges the loss of memory that comes from the unchanging nature of traditional monuments. Through its dependence on time, a counter-monument reveals the limitations of traditional monuments and works against the loss of memory. According to Young, counter-monuments prompt people to "remember for themselves," and thereby avoid presenting a simplified history in the way that a traditional monument often does (1992, 276).

The four pieces in this chapter all draw attention to how war, and the art associated with it, impacts our landscape, whether it is through the creation of traditional monuments and statues as described by Wendy Elliott and Andria Hill-Lehr, the removal of a traditional monument as reflected upon by Angela Henderson, the development of a counter-monument as told by Jessica Lynn Wiebe, or the buildings and geography Peter Dykhuis draws on in his artistic practice.

We begin with Elliott and Hill-Lehr's "Hallowed Ground," which describes the struggle to erect a commemorative statue of Mona Parsons, a Wolfville resident who lived in the German-occupied Netherlands during the Second World War and who was sent to a Nazi work camp because she sheltered Allied airmen. Parsons did not fit the usual profile of figures celebrated for their war work, and the statue of her dancing reflects that difference. It was only after a protracted campaign that her figure now shares the post office lawn in Wolfville with two other war memorials: a traditional commemorative cairn with a plaque inscribed with the names of those who died in the First and Second World Wars, and an oak tree planted from an acorn brought back from England by a First World War veteran. Fittingly, the site of these memorials hosts a weekly peace vigil that started at the beginning of the war in Afghanistan in 2001.

In contrast to Elliott and Hill-Lehr, who focus on creating a memorial, Henderson examines what is left when a commemorative statue is removed. The statue of Edward Cornwallis, erected in 1931 to commemorate the early governor of Nova Scotia, was removed in 2018 following a sustained protest that began in the 1980s. To many, the statue represented a silencing of the Mi'kmaw people and the many injustices—including a bounty on Mi'kmaw lives—that they had suffered at his hands. While the statue has gone, the plinth on which it stood remains, and Henderson uses the artistic technique of frottage, or rubbing, to capture the surface texture of the plinth. She then applies that texture to a page of historic text referring to the use of colonial names in city planning so that parts of the text disappear. Through this artistic practice, she explores how textural erasure offers a place of absence that can act as a productive space of counter-memory.

Wiebe examines both monuments and counter-monuments in "The Space Between: Endurance, Exhaustion, and Remembrance," an account of her performance-based installation that she conducted as part of Uncommon Common Art, a community-wide art exhibition in Kings County, NS, in 2017. Wiebe invited veterans, military members, and civilians to fill sandbags and build a trench wall around the Acadia University War Monument in Wolfville. The site-specific work connected the local history of war in Kings County and current and past sites of conflict with passersby entering a space that echoed the trenches in which so many soldiers fought and thousands died. The installation encouraged participants and viewers to engage with the memorial space and deeply reflect on the names inscribed on the monument, making the memorial, which over time had become invisible in the everyday landscape, visible again.

To close this chapter, Dykhuis's "*Pure War* and Mixed Messages" explores the concept of war and art in a larger context by reflecting on how his parents' experiences in the German-occupied Netherlands during the Second World War, his own interest in flying, and his reading of Paul Virilio's *Pure War* led to an awareness of how local communities are affected by global politics and warfare. This, in turn, prompted his artistic exploration of Halifax as a "pure war" environment as depicted in his work. Dykhuis's work connects to concepts of monuments and counter-monuments through his observations and identification of invisible markers of war in Nova Scotia that are directly or indirectly interrelated to military interests globally.

Our hope is that this chapter on war and art will encourage readers to consider their own communities and the landscapes where they live, work, and play, and reflect on how these spaces are marked directly or indirectly by war. We hope readers will think about the public art they encounter in their daily lives and contemplate how such artworks—monuments or counter-monuments—function as memorials, to ask which stories are being preserved and which are being erased or ignored. Do these pieces invite engagement and reflection, or do they encourage passivity? Artists are driven to record the impact of war, whether it is an attempt to come to terms with the nature and reality of violence or to record something for posterity. We should pay attention to what their works have to say.

Hallowed Ground

Wendy Elliott and Andria Hill-Lehr

TWO MONUMENTS, ONE SPACE

> *In Wolfville, where, until very recently, there were no letterboxes, where there is no mail delivery, the post office is the centre of town. (Wright 1957, 213)*

As the renowned Atlantic Canadian historian, the late Esther Clark Wright, knew so well, in Wolfville, the post office "is the forum, the market place, the exchange. The club. It is the place where you see your friends. If you want to know what is going on in Wolfville, you go to the post office" (1957, 139–40). That may be why there are two monuments at the Wolfville post office.

The first dates to 1920 when the Great War Veterans' Association pressured the town council to raise a memorial to the area's twenty-nine fallen soldiers. A bronze tablet on a stone cairn was dedicated on June 3, 1921. The cairn received "not a little adverse criticism" in the local newspaper, *The Wolfville Acadian*. Veterans led a drive for donations to add a statue, but money was tight. As a result, the bronze figure of the Unknown Soldier sat at the railway freight shed until the entire $1,902.56 bill was paid. Another bronze tablet was then added after 1945, and in the late 1970s, the cairn was upgraded by the Carey family in memory of Corporal Orren W. Carey of Wallbrook.

The second monument on the site, an unofficial one, is an old, gnarled oak tree to the west of the driveway. Alfred Lake, a veteran of the First World War, brought the acorn home. Lake served with the 85th Nova Scotia Battalion and was badly wounded. In England on convalescent leave in 1918, he went to Windsor to see the castle. There was a large, very old oak tree on the grounds, a descendant of the tree in which King Charles I reputedly took refuge at the time of the English Civil War almost two hundred years before. Lake returned home to Wolfville with a few acorns from this "royal oak," which he planted in front of the post office where he was a caretaker. He kept the grounds in immaculate condition while he worked there, and his oak still stands today.

A PLACE OF VIGIL

Between the cairn with its bronze statue standing eternally at attention and the aging oak tree with its twisting branches, the Wolfville Peace Vigil has hoisted its banners above the post office lawn every Saturday at noon since October 13, 2001. Interviewed for the *The Kentville Advertiser* in the aftermath of 9/11, participants hoped their presence might make a difference. "By times we have stood silently," David Mangle states. "Other times we have sung, talked amongst ourselves and with others, distributed literature, made speeches, read poetry, and more" (Elliott 2011).

Maxine Barrett wonders, "As we stand in front of the post office week after week, month after month, year after year, are we making a difference?...I think so," she concludes. "If every person that passes by looks at the banners, the peace activists, and takes a moment to consider our message, then we have made a difference." Bill Zimmerman comments that the vigil "is a visible reminder of Wolfville's long tradition of seeking peace in the world. If we can help people remember that violence isn't the best way to resolve conflicts and spur them to take even a small personal action for peace, we have done a lot" (Elliott 2011).

In its twenty-year history, the Wolfville Peace Vigil has marked several occasions. In 2003, vigil members joined groups in twelve other Maritime communities to protest against the US invasion of Iraq. In

2008, the vigil turned into a rally on the Pan-Canadian Day of Action for US War Resisters. About thirty-five people stood in support of US war resisters, including Wolfville's Raging Grannies, who sang. In 2009, about seventy-five people braved frigid winter winds to attend a climate-change vigil, and in 2011, the vigil turned into a memorial for the late opposition leader Jack Layton.

RECOGNIZING A HEROINE

When Mona Parsons died in Wolfville in 1976, her story lay as if buried in the Acadia University archives. When Andria Hill-Lehr unearthed Parsons's story in the 1990s, details were scant, so she thought a play, *The Bitterest Time*, might encourage those who knew more to come forward. Instead, those who saw it wondered why the story of Parsons's heroism in aiding Allied airmen in German-occupied Netherlands wasn't more widely known. Hill-Lehr soon learned that much more of Parsons's story lay in Europe. Accessing it required a trip that the mother of six could not afford.

Enter Robbins Elliott, the son of Parsons's family doctor. He grew up in Wolfville on Linden Avenue, just around the corner from her. As a young officer in Europe during the final days of the Second World War, he had heard that Parsons had been found close to Germany's border with the Netherlands. On Saturday, April 21, 1945, Elliott wrote to his parents in Wolfville:

> *You probably will be very surprised to know that Mona Parsons Leonhardt is living three doors down with Canadian nurses. After undergoing terrible experiences for harboring Allied airmen in their house near Hilversum, she and her husband were given life sentences by the Germans. Mona was sent to a work camp in a mill near Krefeld. Our bombing forced the Huns to move her camp near Osnabrück, and about three weeks ago she managed to escape during bombardment.... In this German town she is at last among friends. She was looking the worse for her spell of imprisonment, but will soon recover.* (Robbins Elliott fonds, Esther Clark Wright Archives, Acadia University)

Easy for a twenty-four-year-old to say, but Robbins felt strongly enough in his late seventies that he coordinated a trip to the Netherlands with Hill-Lehr to help conduct further research. He believed that a book, along with a documentary film and the already-written play, would eventually provide Parsons with the recognition she deserved.

Hill-Lehr's biography, *Mona Parsons: From Privilege to Prison, from Nova Scotia to Nazi Europe*, came out in 2000 and made a bit of a splash. Parsons's name and that of Wolfville's first female town councillor, Laura Haliburton Moore, were suggested to the local historical society as possible street names. In time, Moore's was accepted, but Parsons's name was somehow besmirched. Apparently, in the minds of some of the old boys' club, she had a drinking problem. Later, the registered nurse who had made regular calls at her home had no qualms saying that liquor wasn't Parsons's problem. PTSD was, as were a number of strokes.

Six years after Hill-Lehr's biography was published, the Women of Wolfville (WOW) took up Parsons's story along with a variety of other female voices in another play, *Matriarchives*. The script resonated with many locally. The next attempt to tangibly recognize Parsons was a request to name the library at Wolfville School after her. After all, the school was built on the site of the Parsons's home. WOW members were informed that the Annapolis Valley Regional School Board didn't do that kind of thing for fear that they would be inundated with requests concerning proposed candidates.

In 2011–12, WOW started a petition to rename Clock Park for Parsons. About three hundred names were collected, and before the town council voted, Sarah Story, an honours history student at Acadia University, made a passionate speech in favour of the name change at the council meeting of May 15, 2012. She suggested that the naming of public spaces should not be a top-down decision made by council. "Generally in the past, financial contributions and political favouritism has trumped and/or negated community input into the naming of public spaces and facilities," she stated, citing the Irvings, Rockefellers, and Carnegies of the world (Elliott 2018). Story noted that most women, not only in Wolfville, but in the larger society, "recognize that our contributions have been often overlooked in the past and/or trumped by the contributions of men and business. We feel that our values, identities, and histories are not adequately reflected in public places—this is why the debate over naming the park has gotten heated at times." Story went on, "It is time women—half of the population of this community—have a space of their own where they can see their gender, values, identities, and contributions be publicly and formally acknowledged and memorialized for women today, and women tomorrow" (Elliott 2018). The all-male town council of the day still voted against the proposal.

Naming a park costs virtually nothing, while commissioning a statue is a costly exercise. However, this was about the only route left to explore for tangible recognition of the war heroine who was virtually unacknowledged in Canada. In 2012, a little band of "statue raisers" reached out to Dutch-born sculptor Nistal Prem de Boer, who has a gift for depicting the human body. When he saw the portrait of Parsons at age nineteen, he wrote, "She is already in my dreams" (Elliott 2018). Soon he was estimating that the sculpture of his imagination might cost \$25,000 or \$30,000. Nistal called the work *The Joy is Almost Too Much to Bear*, words Parsons wrote home once she had reached Holland at the end of the Second World War (Berry 2017). Fundraising began in earnest.

In November 2012, de Boer was ready to begin a scale model maquette. The little bronze maquette was unveiled at the Acadia University Art Gallery in 2014. Following this event, the Wolfville Historical Society provided funds and the Government of Nova Scotia kicked in \$8,000. Elisabeth Kosters, another Dutch native, took on the complex task of applying for money from the federal government's Legacy Fund. In a 2015 appeal to the Wolfville town council, Kosters noted that her motivation came from the fact that Parsons "did what my aunt and my mom did: she hid Allied pilots. And for that act of resistance, she was sentenced to death and later to life in prison. She spent four years in a concentration camp, and I have no doubt that she was severely traumatized the rest of her life without anyone recognizing that" (2015).

Kosters found de Boer's design for the memorial "utterly moving: it shows her in rags on old wooden shoes, dancing wildly—because she is free. The image conveys the very idea of freedom, something we take for granted too easily." For Kosters, the sculpture pays "tribute to all those forgotten and unknown women who—in their own way—resisted injustice, dictatorship and terror." By placing a sculpture in a prominent place, she said, "we would recognize that Canadian liberators also benefited from those who worked in the background, in the hidden folds of the war: women who didn't question risking their lives for justice and against terror" (2015).

Dr. Allen Eaves, a Vancouver resident with roots in the Annapolis Valley, jumped on board readily as a major donor, and, as a result of CBC's coverage of the fundraising drive on Remembrance Day in 2015, small meaningful gifts came in from all across Canada. Some donors were veterans of the Second World War, perhaps even stationed in the Netherlands, their shaky handwriting betraying their age, and some had had family members stationed there. One recalled that Parsons's courage and resourcefulness in getting across enemy lines were well known to the staff of the Canadian embassy in the Netherlands after the war.

The federal funds were approved late in 2016 and de Boer went off to China to supervise the casting. When it was delivered to Wolfville, town staff installed the sculpture under Alfred Lake's oak tree on the post office's west lawn. On May 5, 2017, which is both the anniversary of the liberation of Holland and of the date on which Parsons penned the words "the joy is almost too much to bear," her sculpture was unveiled. There was, finally, a tangible memorial in recognition of her heroism. Songs were sung, and all the right speeches were

Figure 7. Sculptor Nistal Prem de Boer's depiction of Wolfville's war heroine Mona Parsons, titled The Joy is Almost Too Much to Bear. (PHOTO BY WENDY ELLIOTT)

made at that celebration, but what many remember was the children picking yellow dandelions and carefully laying them at the feet of the sculpture.

Years ago, had there been a street or park named after Mona Parsons, Wolfville would not have been half as excited. It would have been far easier for this to have happened, but having inherited some of Parsons's determination, we have been glad to witness the installation of her sculpture and to share with all Nova Scotians the story of the only Canadian civilian woman to be imprisoned by the Nazis.

Some would say Wolfville has three monuments on the lawn of its post office: a war memorial to recall the many that time might forget, an historic oak planted by a veteran, and a sculpture honouring a war heroine whose resistance activities were also carried out by thousands of others whose names we will never know. These monuments make for a sacred place—one worthy of a peace vigil.

Figure 8. The Wolfville Peace Vigil continues on the lawn of the Wolfville post office even through the winter. The vigil began before the US invasion of Iraq in 2003 and takes place every Saturday at noon. (PHOTO BY WENDY ELLIOTT)

(untitled)

Angela Henderson

Situated in a small park in front of Halifax's railway station, a monument made in the likeness of Edward Cornwallis was erected in 1931 to pay tribute to the so-called founding father of Halifax, a military figure who imposed the British rule of law in Mi'kma'ki, the ancestral and unceded territory of the Mi'kmaq. This bronze statue was funded by the Canadian National Railway primarily to promote tourism. Appointed Governor of Nova Scotia, Cornwallis infamously issued what is now known as the Scalping Proclamation, a bounty offered in 1749 for anyone who killed a Mi'kmaw adult or child. The establishment of this monument, along with streets, schools, and towns bearing the name of colonial leaders who incited genocide, embodies the pervasive violence of colonization throughout Turtle Island. The statue was an ongoing source of contention and a rallying point for protests over the past four decades. In 2018, Halifax Regional Council decided that the bronze statue was to be removed and put into storage, leaving a vacant granite plinth as a poignant, unintentional "anti-monument," reminding us of the necessity of reconciling this difficult history. This project explores urban naming conventions that glorify figures of colonial expansion and project a "founders' ideology" onto our public landscape. Stripped of its role as a site of commemoration, the plinth that once supported the figure of Cornwallis becomes available as a site for examining how absence can serve as a powerful condition for acknowledging the traumas of colonization.

On a plinth with no monument, I placed a text written by amateur historians lauding the colonial nomenclature of civic spaces throughout Halifax. The textural remains on this granite stone are used as a substrate for frottage, through which a gestural mapping of the plinth takes place. Using the plinth's topography of gaps and voids, the frottage further distorts and destabilizes the letterforms to reveal a fragmented text on the opposite side of the page. The flux of presence and erasure in this sculptural text identifies the plinth as a provocative space for imagining new narratives within the absence of the colonial figure.

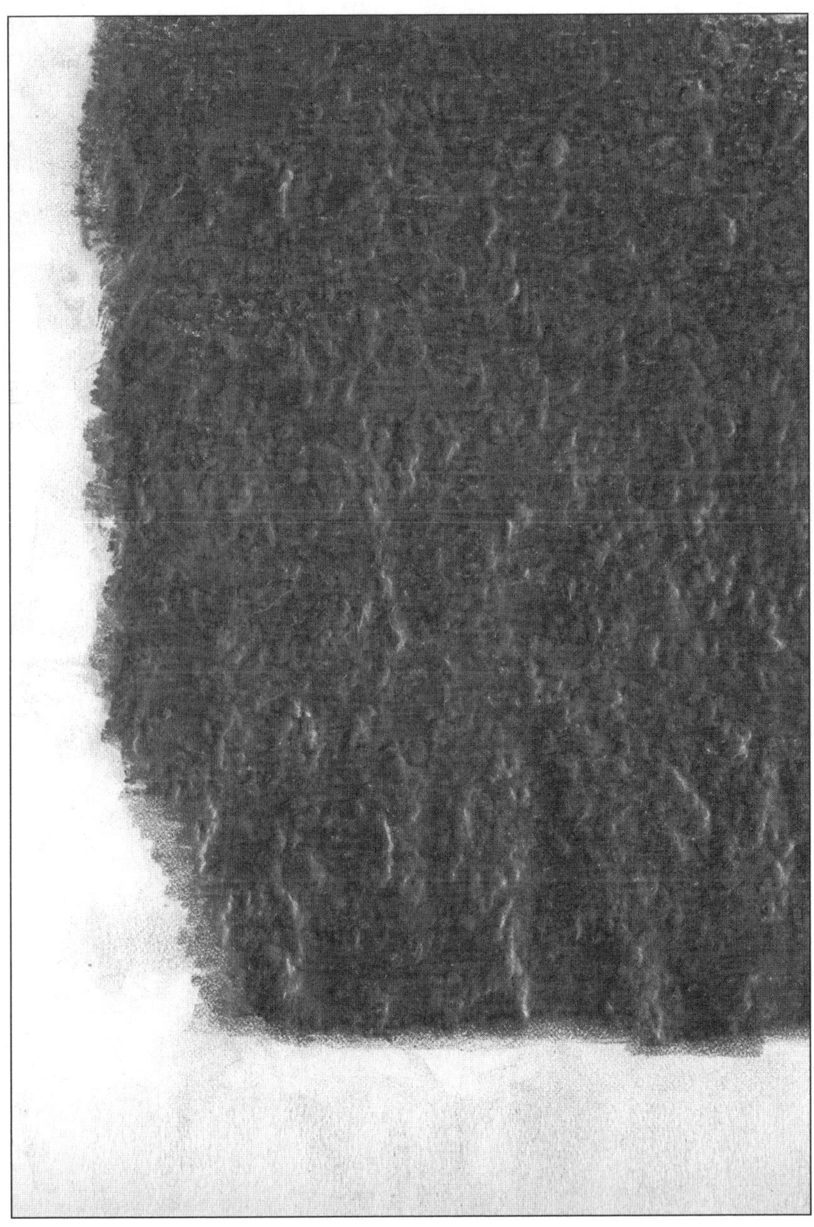

Figure 9. Graphite frottage of granite plinth, southwest corner. Henderson, Angela. (untitled), *2019.* (PHOTO BY ANGELA HENDERSON)

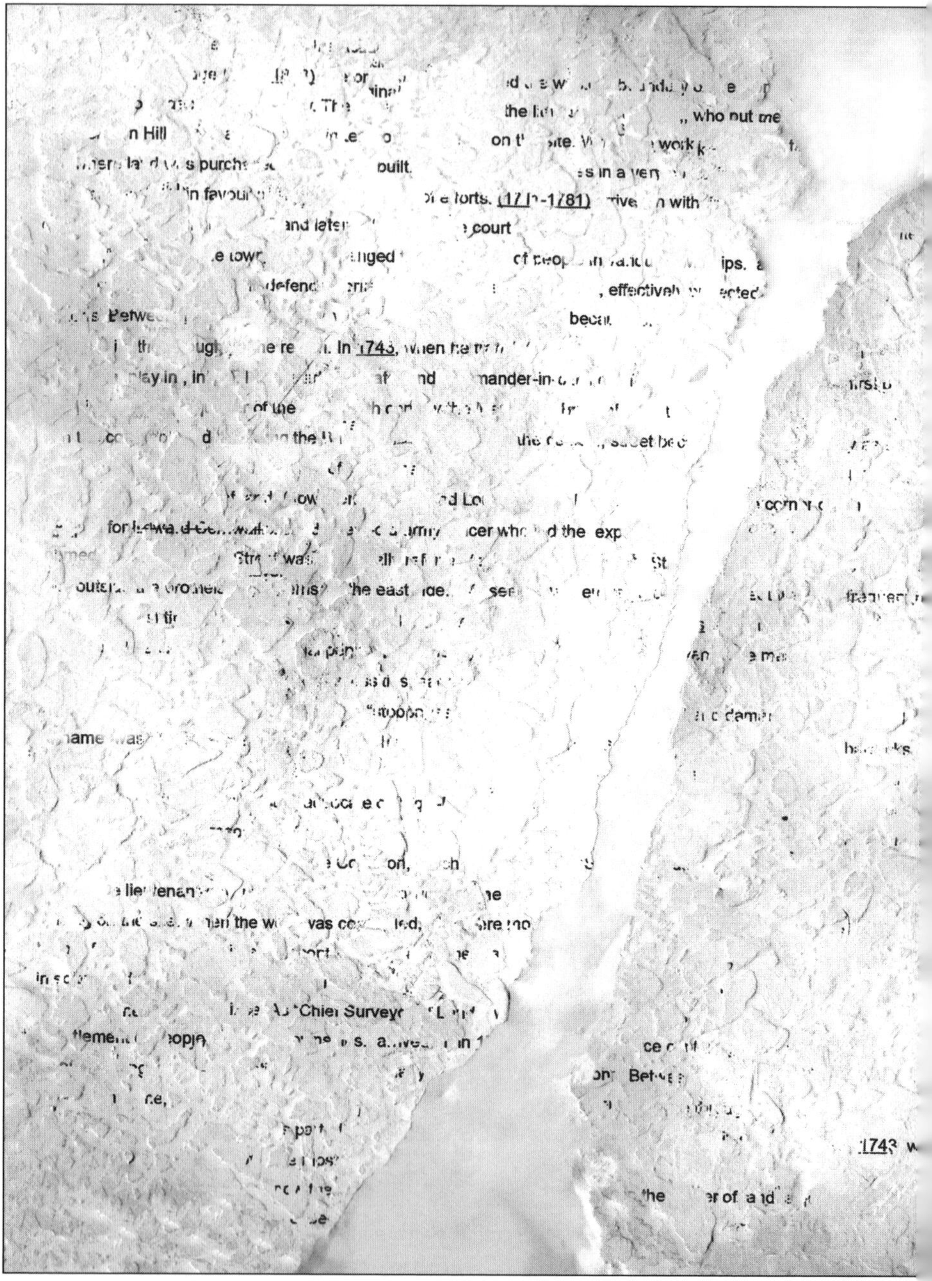

who put me
n Hill
purch
built.
in favour
(1771-1781)
court
effectively
In 1743, when
mander-in-
for Edward Cornwallis
the east side.
the lieutenant
vas completed,
Chief Surveyor
1743

Figure 10: in situ. Henderson, Angela. (untitled), *2019.* (PHOTO BY ANGELA HENDERSON)

Figure 11. Graphite frottage of granite plinth, northeast corner. Henderson, Angela. (untitled), *2019.* (PHOTO BY ANGELA HENDERSON)

The Space Between: Endurance, Exhaustion, and Remembrance

Jessica Lynn Wiebe

THE INITIAL CONCEPT

As a veteran, I have often thought about the physical weight soldiers carry throughout their training and overseas deployments and the emotional weight they continue to carry long after. My focus on this idea led to a performance work in 2014, in which I lifted and moved fourteen heavy sandbags. I did not allow myself to move forward until I had moved all of the sandbags with me. Eventually, I left the sandbags and continued, carrying only two. I wanted to show that you can let go but that you will always carry something of that weight with you, and that's okay.

Drawn to ideas of endurance, exhaustion, and remembrance, I began to conceive of a project in which I might carry a heavy concrete sandbag through a landscape over a period of time, leaving it somewhere significant as a memorial. However, I did not have a landscape, a distance, a concrete sandbag, or a reason why.

Then, in 2016, Uncommon Common Art (UCA) released a call for artists to propose projects that drew upon the rich geology, history, and possible futures of Kings County, seeking art installations that framed the landscape through concepts of the terrestrial and subterranean. I now had a landscape and a starting point. It was through the intersection of landscape, military history, and community participation that this project developed into a temporary performance-based installation: a counter-monument.

My early research led me to Camp Aldershot. The Canadian Armed Forces base played a significant role during both world wars, training thousands of soldiers from across Nova Scotia before they were deployed to Europe, transported by the Dominion Atlantic Railway through Kings County. Camp Aldershot, with its barren sand dunes, provides a landscape well-suited for drills and manoeuvres, preparing soldiers for the extreme conditions they might face in combat zones. I decided that I would sculpt a concrete sandbag, using sand and gravel from Camp Aldershot, and carry the sculpture along the former railroad tracks to the Acadia University War Monument in Wolfville.

This physical gesture of endurance, exhaustion, and remembrance would quite literally link the landscape of Kings County to the story I wanted to tell. The distance between Aldershot and Wolfville is close to the standard military Battle Fitness Test of thirteen kilometres. During this standard march, soldiers are required to carry a fifty-five-pound rucksack. The concrete sandbag would weigh the same. Carrying the concrete sandbag along this route would symbolically tie the performance to the soldiers' training and transportation through this landscape on their way to Halifax before deployment to Europe. It would embody the physical exhaustion and nervous energy soldiers feel when going to war and not knowing—or knowing—what they will face.

At the memorial space, I envisioned building a recognizable element of war: a trench wall of military standard sandbags along the front edge of the retaining wall below the monument, with the concrete sandbag sitting on the top of this trench wall between the two columns. At the end of UCA's temporary public art exhibition, I would return the sand to Camp Aldershot. The trench wall would be emblematic of the deep trench systems of the First and Second World Wars as well as the architecture of war in areas from Korea to Afghanistan, from the grainy black-and-white photographs of First World War soldiers to the contemporary photographs and video footage of beige sea containers with sandbags, concrete and wire-mesh

HESCO barriers, and bunkers—places where soldiers spend hours, days, and months living and surviving.

COUNTER-MONUMENTS

When my project was accepted, Angela Henderson, the curator of UCA 2017, introduced me to the term *counter-monument*. Following our conversation, I read many papers on the counter-monument movement in Europe. I became familiar with how academics, architects, and artists were actively engaging with the complex realities of memorial spaces and seeking how contemporary memorial spaces and counter-monuments can engage and bring viewers into the space where they must make an effort to interpret the multiple meanings of the memorial. Understanding this concept gave me the language to express my initial idea. As monuments tend to merge with the landscape over time, they become invisible. With this work, I wanted to disrupt the invisibility of the memorial space of the war monument and the experience of war that it embodied. I wanted people to engage with the space and read the names inscribed on its pillars.

THE PROCESS: THE SANDBAG WORK PARTY(IES)

This project was incredibly labour intensive and required a lot of strategic planning. I had to get permission and clearance from range control at Camp Aldershot before I could organize a sandbag work party to fill sandbags on the training grounds. I invited veterans, serving military members, and civilians to join me in filling and transporting 250 sandbags. After the day was over, my father-in-law asked me what the purpose was of building a trench wall against an existing retaining wall. We discussed possible solutions that would invite passersby to engage with the memorial space. I thought about the spaces in which soldiers lived overseas: the concrete barriers, bunkers, sea containers, towers, and so on. I wanted to incorporate the poetics of those spaces into this work.

That night I created a new sketch. I decided to build the makeshift trench wall around the monument, leaving two ends open for viewers to enter and leave. This worked twofold. The monument embodied the experience of war, and the design would symbolically place the monument, and the passerby, back into the trenches in which so many soldiers died. I hoped the experience would encourage people to consider the names inscribed on the monument more thoughtfully. I then calculated the thickness and length of the new trench walls and realized that I would need at least four hundred more sandbags. I arranged a second sandbag work party. I experienced the endurance and exhaustion I had intended to capture in the process. However, bringing people together to fill and transport 650 sandbags reminded me of the camaraderie that is so present in the military. It felt good to again be part of something larger than myself.

THE PROCESS: SCULPTING THE CONCRETE SANDBAG

While I initially intended to sculpt just one concrete sandbag, this was the first time I had worked with cement. Through trial and error, I ended up sculpting not one, but many concrete sandbags. I mixed and poured cement directly into the military-grade sandbags. At first, the sandbags were too perfect in shape, so I began to rip holes in the bags to allow the cement to bulge out as I filled them. I would then shape the cement into a more organic form. Limp, torn, and broken, the sculptures began to look more corporeal and more suggestive of the physical loss of life than the square granite blocks of the existing monument.

THE PERFORMANCE

On May 25, 2017, I invited military and civilian communities from across Nova Scotia to march along the Dominion Atlantic Railway tracks, from Camp Aldershot to the Acadia University War Monument. I carried the fifty-five-pound concrete sandbag in my rucksack while others carried day packs with water, and two military members carried their heavy rucksacks. Along the route, veterans, serving military members, and local civilians shared stories of how their lives had been impacted by the military and war. By the time we reached the war monument, my feet were burning from the march, but people were waiting for us, and I had to focus on the task at hand. The day before, we had stacked the 650 sandbags in a pile beside the monument. I now instructed the participants on how to build the makeshift trench, placing the concrete sandbags sporadically throughout. The physical effort consumed participants like a meditation: moving sandbag by sandbag, slamming them into place, stomping them down, pressing by hand to adjust the positioning, and thoughtfully repeating. Finally, I pulled the concrete sandbag from my rucksack and placed it on top of the trench wall between the two pillars, bridging the space between.

CONCLUSION

This project revealed to me that the monument is not the memorial. The memorial exists in the space between the viewer and the monument, and a counter-monument can reimagine a pre-existing monument and engage passersby to reflect within this memorial space. Throughout the sandbag work parties, the performance, and the five-month duration of the installation, this project fostered dialogue about the military, war, and memory in this region and abroad. The very temporal nature of this project made a monument that had become invisible once again visible, the removal and absence of the temporary trench wall once again revealing the monument so that it will—for some time at least—continue to be seen.

Can art bridge the gap between military experience and civilian understanding of that experience? I don't know. What I do know is that art can encourage viewers to engage with a particular space and to make an effort to understand the layered meanings. By bringing the past and present together through the embodiment of endurance, exhaustion, and remembrance, this work created a social space for public reflection and dialogue about the complex meaning of memorial spaces and the making of memory.

Figure 12. Installation, sandbags, sand, and concrete. Wiebe, Jessica Lynn. The Space Between, *2017.* (PHOTO BY ERNEST CADEGAN)

Figure 13. Sandbag Work Party 2. Wiebe, Jessica Lynn. The Space Between, *2017.* (PERFORMANCE STILL BY JESSICA LYNN WIEBE)

Figure 14. Performance. Wiebe, Jessica Lynn. The Space Between, *2017.*
(PERFORMANCE STILL BY ERNEST CADEGAN)

Pure War and Mixed Messages

Peter Dykhuis

WAR

After surviving five years of Nazi occupation during the Second World War, my parents arrived in Canada in 1948 as Dutch immigrants. My father's family owned a farm in the northern province of Groningen; my mother's family were tenant farmers in the neighbouring province and were Frisians, an ethnically and linguistically unique people. They settled in London, ON, where I was born.

At home, we spoke English as my parents, Geert and Martje, now George and Martha, were determined to assimilate the family into "Canadian" culture. Dutch and Frisian were spoken at family gatherings when the "old folk" relaxed among themselves. Or when my parents communicated together about private matters that excluded my sister and myself. They also spoke at family gatherings in hushed tones about the war: who did what to whom; who was to be trusted, even in their Dutch Calvinist community; who was identified as Nazi sympathizers, or worse, collaborators.

My mother's family had harboured Jewish people who had fled the southern cities to "disappear" into the rural landscape. Spies and informants were everywhere, and the punishment was cruel—if caught offering refuge to Jews, Dutch families were sent to the camps with them. My father's family, since they owned their farm, squirrelled away food for themselves that was otherwise earmarked for the

Nazis. They also modified the architecture of their barn and created secret spaces behind the hay bales to hide Allied aviators who had fallen from the sky. This was an enormous risk. When discovered with Allied airmen on their premises, families were summarily executed, their livestock confiscated, and their houses and barns razed by fire.

WAR AND AVIATION

My parents, at that time boyfriend and girlfriend in a relationship defined by war and Nazi curfews, often recalled that there was a constant drone overhead as waves of British bomber squadrons flew over at night and American bombers went over by day. This was augmented by the clatter of aerial machine-gun and cannon fire and flaming bombers and fighter planes falling dramatically from the sky.

On December 11, 1943, my father witnessed a major aerial battle. He watched as a damaged Boeing B-17 Flying Fortress drifted below its group formation, its crew still managing to shoot down three German fighter planes before they bailed from their doomed bomber. My father's family hid Edwin Pollock, the American pilot of that B-17, for over a week as he recovered from wounds resulting from his parachute jump. Once healthy to travel, he was linked up with the next safe house operated by the Dutch underground resistance fighters.

My father's family were not the only heroes I knew. My first wife's father, Theo Anema, had been a bombardier/navigator of a B-17 with the US Air Force and a decorated operator of a Pathfinder system, an early version of aerial radar. He flew thirty-one missions before his plane was shot down over (then) Yugoslavia. Theo jumped from his doomed aircraft with a wounded waist gunner, pulling the gunner's parachute ripcord before free-falling farther to then parachute to earth. Fortunately, Theo was returned to the Allied forces by the Yugoslavian Partisans. Post-war, he went on to become a "mad man" in Chicago's advertising business and create the wholesome commercial image of the Jolly Green Giant.

While I never knew John Wark, my father-in-law, as he passed away before I met his daughter Jayne, he was also an aviator in the Second World War, flying reconnaissance missions in (then) Burma. We only have photos and stories of his wartime service, though his family is undertaking research in attempts to reveal his full story.

CENTRAL AIRWAYS

With stories of rescued Allied airmen buzzing in my ears, my father and I would go to the London airport on Sunday afternoons to watch airplanes come and go. In 1966, when I was ten years old, I was finally able to board an aircraft for the first time as part of a family trip to the Netherlands: the propeller-driven Vickers Viscount from London to Toronto, the larger Vickers Vanguard to Montréal, and then the crème de la crème of contemporary aviation at that time, a Douglas DC-8 jetliner to Schiphol, Amsterdam. The last leg was a non-stop flight and a luxury at that time.

During that trip, I met my grandfather and namesake, staying in his house on the Jonkersvaart outside of the town of De Wilp. I also saw the hidden room in the hayloft of the barn that was the secret place to harbour the Allied aviators.

Gainfully employed by the Art Gallery of Ontario in 1983 and obsessed with these aviation stories, I pursued training for a private pilot's licence from Central Airways on Toronto Island. I proved to be an astute pilot, completing my training in less than the normal time and soloing in a Cessna 150 after only fifteen hours of training. I credited my ability to the time spent in art school engaged with contour drawing, exercises that promote the link between visual perception and eye-hand coordination. I also designed and installed travelling exhibitions for the Art Gallery of Ontario and knew a thing or two about what was level and what was not, a very important baseline in flying an airplane!

I recreationally flew out of Toronto Island Airport until I moved to Nova Scotia in 1991. I attained a rating for the larger four-seat Cessna 172 and added night certification with instrument training to my ticket. It is one of the most exciting things I have accomplished. Aviation and flying, along with reading spatial images of weather phenomena, fully inform my art practice about how to map and visualize geographic territories.

PAUL VIRILIO AND *PURE WAR*

In 1984, as a recreational pilot and budding visual artist in Toronto, I read *Pure War*, an interview with French cultural theorist Paul Virilio by Sylvère Lotringer. In it, Virilio sketches out how the global post–Second World War and Cold War economies were on perpetual war footings that dedicated entire military-industrial cultures to instant nuclear launch and speedy armed retaliation. As such, global military machines and their support economies had to be constantly primed and ready for action, even if it implied mutual assured destruction.

As I discovered, "domestic" suppliers such as Ford, General Motors, Boeing, and Honeywell were entangled in this process; not just the dedicated military corporations such as Lockheed Martin, General Dynamics, Raytheon, and L3, to name a few.

***PURE WAR* AND HALIFAX**

After moving to Bedford in 1991, I was a first-time homeowner with small children, and had no financial resources for recreational flying. However, as an aviation nerd, I paid attention to the aircraft overhead and noticed the military Lockheed T-33 jet trainers and Lockheed P-3 Orion surveillance aircraft that left each morning from Royal Canadian Air Force Base Shearwater to patrol the North Atlantic in search of Russian submarines. And when I rode the early morning buses into Halifax, I often shared seats with enlisted members of the navy, including submariners who had the privilege to sport beards while preparing for missions.

Bedford, a neighbourhood carved out of a hard-rock Cambrian geology, relied on dynamite blasting to make space for house construction. Consequently, for years, I did not correctly interpret the booming noises coming from the horizon. I finally realized that the distinct rhythmic popping sounds that I often heard in the distance had nothing to do with real estate and was the report of gunfire from Bedford Rifle Range, part of CFB Halifax, where military forces conduct live ammunition training. It was then that I realized that Halifax represented a "pure war" economy as posited by Virilio.

In the year 2000, I began to track where military suppliers were located and produced artworks that vaguely mapped them. Only recently—in the first stage of my new 2019 project titled *Stars and Scopes (The Powers That Be)*—have I pinpointed, using the ever-available Google Maps application (the civilian by-product of military satellite surveillance technology), their precise urban locations, including US corporations such as Lockheed Martin, General Dynamics, and L3, with their Canadian counterparts, IMP Aerospace & Defence, and Irving Shipbuilding.

It should be noted that, when awarded the contract to build the next generation of combat ships for the Canadian navy in 2011, Irving Shipbuilding was contracted to build the "empty" vessels, which were then weaponized with military combat systems provided by the likes of Lockheed Martin and General Dynamics. From my point of view, "pure war" is on full display in Halifax—but hiding in plain sight to most of my fellow citizens. It became my mission to reveal, through cultural expression, the military interests that were camouflaged in the social, political, and economic fabric of Halifax.

MIXED MESSAGES

Combining a field of mundane domestic messages collected at home and at work with the ominous silhouette of an F/A-18 Hornet, *Mixed Messages* (2006) alludes to the "pure war" theories of Virilio that articulate the interweave between military interests and domestic economies. Each banal note addressed to me, the artist, functions as a micro-narrative grounded against the silhouette of the meta-narrative of symbolic, aggressive military power. At the time, Canadian ground forces in Afghanistan were deployed in combat duty beyond their more traditional peacekeeping missions for the first time in decades.

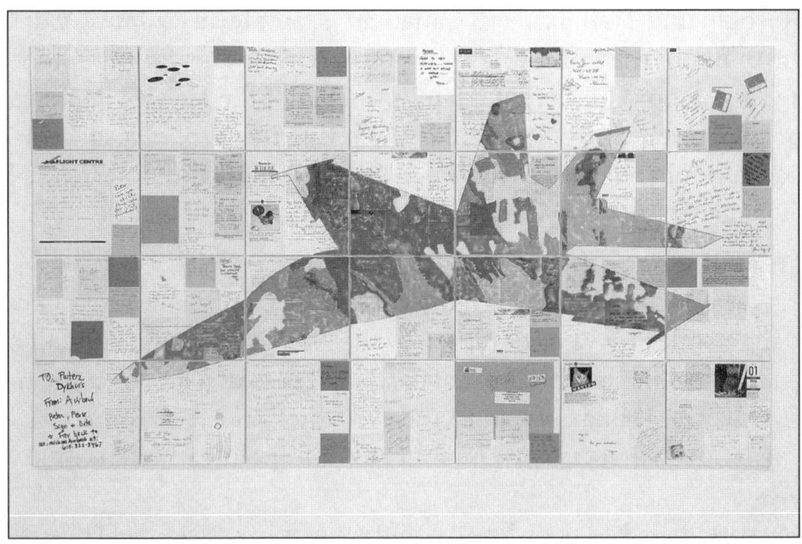

Figure 15. Encaustic on collaged messages/notes on 28 panels, 48” x 84” installed. Dykhuis, Peter. Mixed Messages, *2006.* (PHOTO BY STEVE FARMER)

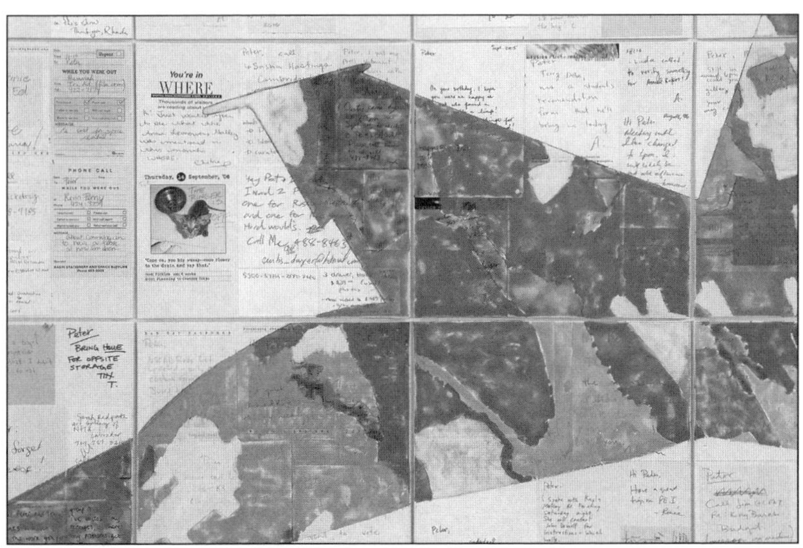

Figure 16. Detail of encaustic on collaged messages/notes on 28 panels, 48” x 84” installed. Dykhuis, Peter. Mixed Messages, *2006.* (PHOTO BY STEVE FARMER)

Recognizing Halifax as a Canadian example of a "pure war" environment, the camouflage pattern within the fighter plane image is a representation of a land-use map of the Halifax Regional Municipality and surrounding area. As posited by Virilio, local economies and inhabitants are always directly or indirectly interrelated with global politics and warfare.

MIXED THOUGHTS

During the Second World War, my parents' lives, socially, economically, and politically, were controlled by the Nazi Wehrmacht. Although not under the immediate threat of death and destruction, our contemporary lives in Halifax, when factoring in the context of "pure war," are also affected socially, economically, and politically by military interests.

My parents risked their lives with their acts of resistance. Thus far without risk of personal injury, through research and art production that represents a quiet resistance of its own, I am able to call out the powers that be.

Conclusion: Weaving Communities Together Through Storytelling

Reina Green, Maya Eichler, and Tracy Moniz

In compiling this collection of stories about war and peace in Nova Scotia, our intention was to gather stories from communities that have been marginalized, unheard, or ignored, and to set them alongside better-known accounts. We wanted to invite people from a range of Nova Scotian communities to tell their stories of the far-ranging and unexpected consequences of war and peace, in their own voices. We also wanted to explore the connections between their stories to identify common threads and opportunities for connection. For example, we find a shared resilience in those who experienced the Halifax Explosion and those who have been forced from their homes because of war in more recent times. We see the sacrifice of both military personnel and the women who have rescued and sheltered others in war-torn countries. We hear of the fight for recognition of those who were denied entry into the military and those who were pushed out of it.

The philosopher Roland Barthes describes text as "a tissue, a woven fabric" (1977, 159). This metaphor, with its reference to weaving, is particularly apt for considering how all the stories in this collection are woven together and for examining what patterns they might share. Weaving is not limited to the creation of fabric and stories; it is also a traditional method of basketmaking in many Indigenous cultures, including Mi'kmaw culture, as is reflected in Catherine Martin's story and her sister's lyrics for "Basketmaker."

Indigenous scholar Sherry Pictou also draws on basket weaving and storytelling in her work, noting that the concept of basket weaving reveals "taken-for-granted strands or relations (splints) and how they are interwoven (interrelated) together, constituting the research journey (basket) as a whole" (2017, 15). Building on these insights about the significance of weaving and storytelling, we see the importance of creating community-engaged knowledge and building community through storytelling, while recognizing the challenges and contradictions contained in such a project. We offer a few thoughts on the common threads and patterns we see as we read the stories collected in this volume in relation to one another, and we encourage you to find other patterns of your own in them.

PLACE AND DISPLACEMENT

The role of military conflict in shaping Nova Scotia as a place—the impact on the province's landscape and culture—is rarely considered. The history of the province, even its very name—*New Scotland*—is rooted in displacement, a displacement most often due to military conflict. Nova Scotia's history belies the national myth of Canada as peacemaker. Part of Mi'kma'ki, Nova Scotia was claimed and named by European settlers, displacing the Indigenous Peoples and erasing much of their history and culture. As El Jones and Susan M. Brigham note in their contributions, the early history of Nova Scotia, and Canada as a whole, focuses on the bravery of the European settlers and ignores the cultural genocide of the Indigenous nations and the violent treatment of Black people. Displacement continued with the Acadian Deportation which began in 1755 and has carried on, reflecting military conflicts happening here and elsewhere ever since. Military personnel and their families have moved in and out of the region: troops have increased the population of Halifax while they awaited transport overseas, as in the First and Second World Wars, and while their families have temporarily made a home on one military base, then another. In addition, peace activists have moved here to avoid conscription into a war they opposed as highlighted by the story of Roger Davies, and for centuries, from the Loyalists onwards, refugees fleeing wars and persecution have found a home here.

Not only have war and peace shaped the history and culture of Nova Scotia, but it has also shaped the landscape and even its soundscape as Peter Dykhuis notes in the chapter on war and art. Shaped by the Halifax Explosion, which saw one community—Richmond—razed and another—the Hydrostone—built, the Halifax skyline is dominated by Citadel Hill, and the city continues to be home to the largest military base in Canada. Military installations and monuments recognizing military events dot the Nova Scotian landscape. Even as these geographic markers of a military presence record the impact of war and peace on Nova Scotia's history, they also exclude and erase other experiences, as Susan M. Brigham, Barbara Lounder, and Angela Henderson observe.

EXCLUSION AND INVISIBILITY

Displacement inevitably leads to being shut out and excluded. That is not the only cause of exclusion as many of the stories in this collection reveal. The history of Nova Scotia has repeatedly silenced Indigenous and Black voices, as shown in Sylvia Parris-Drummond's account of her father's experience in the No. 2 Construction Battalion (also known as the Black Battalion) and Don Julien's description of Mi'kmaw war veterans. Other communities also fought to be included, as shown in Gregory Kennedy's history of Acadians in the Canadian Expeditionary Force. More recently, exclusion has been experienced by the 2SLGBTQIA+ community through the Canadian Government's LGBT Purge, as well as by women barred from combat roles in the Canadian military until 1989. In addition, memorialization regularly excludes those who do not fit the conventional profile of a war hero. Wendy Elliott and Andria Hill-Lehr describe the long fight to have a statue of Mona Parsons erected in Wolfville because she did not fit a traditional model. Those involved in peace activism have also been excluded, often shamed for their stance. Maya Eichler writes of Mary Russell Chesley and the later Pugwash Conferences, and kathrin winkler recounts the history of the Nova Scotia chapter of the Voice of Women for Peace. These accounts demonstrate the province's long history of peace activism that is often overwritten by its military history. Such peace activism continues into the present and includes, for example, an annual protest against the Halifax Security Forum and weekly peace vigils in Wolfville.

Invisibility is often reflected in whether and how the contributions of certain communities are acknowledged. The vital work of the Canadian Forestry Corps and the Black Battalion in the First World War goes unremarked, despite its importance in clearing forests, building roads, and defusing mines. Also unseen—and unpaid—is the work of military spouses, most of them women, which allows the military to continue to function in the way it does. This reality is explored in the pieces by Deborah Norris, Catherine Littler, and Leigh Spanner. Military spouses take on additional childcare and household responsibilities and often put their own careers on hold as they move from base to base, supporting their partners even as they "work them out and work them in."

BELONGING AND COMMUNITY

There is no question that military conflict has displaced, excluded, and rendered invisible certain communities. A brief investigation into Canada's military history underscores this, as Susan M. Brigham and Claudine Bonner observe in the chapter on African Nova Scotian communities. About the concept of Canada as a peacekeeper and a cultural mosaic, Brigham writes, "Such national narratives idealize a Canada that allows some citizens to feel at home and others to feel like they do not belong." The experiences of the African Nova Scotian, Acadian, and Mi'kmaw communities bear this out, as does that of the 2SLGBTQIA+ community. At the same time, military experience can build new forms of belonging. Veterans note the sense of community among military personnel due to the intense socialization they undergo, even as they are uprooted from their hometowns and families and often struggle to reintegrate back into civilian society when they leave military service. As John Whelan says, "There is no going back to who I was before the military." While members may have a strong sense of belonging within the Canadian Armed Forces, the bond is tenuous—shifting with each deployment and move from base to base. Moreover, for those who are forced to leave the military, whether due to injury or circumstances such as the LGBT Purge, the sudden loss of community can be overwhelming. Some connect with or advocate for other groups and causes, as Darl Wood has done with peace activism and feminism, as Frank Letourneau has done with Pride, and as Giff Gifford did with Veterans Against Nuclear Arms. Others, like Jessica Miller with the Veteran Farm Project, work to create a sense of belonging for veterans as they reintegrate into civilian society upon release from the military.

Military conflict brings disparate communities together, as Don Julien notes in his conversation with Jenna Stewart about Mi'kmaw veterans serving in the First World War. As he points out, the war "opened a lot of doors for friendship" as soldiers depended on each other "regardless of their race or where they were from." Unfortunately, those friendships did not always last when people returned to their home communities. Military conflict also brings service personnel and those in war-torn communities together through shared experience. Ken Hoffer notes the impact of seeing the killing fields in East Timor and recognizing how he and the rest of the crew of HMCS *Protecteur* were there to help the inhabitants recover and rebuild. Refugees uprooted from their home communities because of military conflict know well the sacrifices entailed, including leaving loved ones behind, as Amara Bangura, Nareen Haj Ali, and Viyan Ali have done, or giving up their work to improve conditions in their home country, as in the case of Marianela Fuertes. They, like military personnel, experience instability as they flee their homes, perhaps to refugee camps, where there is a sense of tenuous belonging and of dislocation, before they have to integrate into yet another new and unfamiliar society.

Recognizing the importance of belonging to a community often drives those involved to build up that community through their own contributions. The nature of their participation can vary widely as this collection demonstrates and may include everything from providing food boxes to veterans to caring for the sick and injured, fighting for human rights, joining peace movements, and creating art to memorialize the effects of war. Many artists, peace activists, refugees, and military veterans are deeply invested in their communities and strengthen their sense of belonging through their contributions.

ADAPTATION AND RESILIENCE

The impact of war can be devastating on all involved. Not only can it ravage a geographic area—as the Halifax Explosion did—but it also destroys people's connections to that place and to one another. In addition, war can demonstrate the human capacity for adaptation and resilience. The stories in this collection are a testament to that strength. Service personnel and veterans experience alienation from civilian society, just as refugees are separated from their home communities. Still, their narratives repeatedly display resilience and the ability to adapt to their shifting circumstances. The immediate effect of military conflict might be destruction, but what follows is rebuilding. This may be physical, involving bricks and mortar as with the building of the Hydrostone neighbourhood in Halifax, described by Paige Farah, or the creation of a memorial to mark the event, as John deWolf explains. Equally, the rebuilding may be social and emotional, as through the Veterans Farm Project and the Canadian Red Cross program "A Story to Tell and a Place for the Telling." As Catherine Baillie Abidi explains, the program offered refugees a safe space to tell of their experiences and help them build a life—and community connections—in Canada. Adaptation and resilience are also evident in the experiences of military families described by Catherine Littler and Deborah Norris. Here, we see families adapting to the deployment of the military member and showing resilience when coping with crises without spousal or parental support.

AN INVITATION

This collection expands beyond the dominant military history of Nova Scotia to demonstrate the multiplicity of stories and the variety of communities impacted by war and peace. It is vital that we create a safe space for these stories to be told—for everyone to tell their story. Those without such a space remain outsiders in their own province. We must listen and recognize the value of all voices. In his discussion of the work of the Army Museum, Ken Hynes emphasizes the importance of commemorating our history. While he focuses on traditional monuments and ceremonies, Jessica Lynn Wiebe and other artists focus on keeping our memories alive through counter-memorials. It is not enough to erect a stone or statue. We need to speak and hear of experiences as told in the narratives gathered here. It is only through learning more about all of our histories that we can prepare for the future. As Barbara Lounder says in her discussion of the Halifax Explosion: "If there is much to learn about the explosion, there is even more to uncover about the risk of another disaster in the future."

We close this collection with an invitation for you to join the conversation, to think about the impact of these stories on you and how your story might connect with each of them. Consider tracing your own patterns in the threads you see shining through these stories. Reflecting on the full view evoked through the lyrics in "Basketmaker" shared in this collection by Catherine Martin—"up and down, in and out, all around"—we ask, "What thoughts have you as you sit so silently?"

Acknowledgements

Most of all, we would like to thank our contributors, without whom this book would not have been possible. Thank you for sharing your stories and for working with us to bring this book to life. This book grew out of the work of the Mount Network for Community-Engaged Research on War and Peace (NCERW). We thank all the members of NCERW, who collectively over the past eight years helped shape the path that led to this collection of stories. In 2016, NCERW organized a workshop on community stories of war and peace, and we thank the participants of that workshop for prompting the ideas that led to the making of this volume. We are grateful to Charlotte Kiddell who was instrumental in organizing that 2016 workshop. In 2017, several NCERW members contributed to a public speakers' series at the Keshen-Goodman branch of the Halifax Public Libraries, which helped move us further in the direction of this collection. We are particularly grateful to Mary O'Brien who helped with editing the first full draft of the manuscript. Raya P. Morrison did the heavy lifting of getting the manuscript edited and ready for publication, for which we are immensely grateful. Thank you, too, to Angela Mombourquette, non-fiction editor at Nimbus Publishing, who championed getting this collection into print. Finally, we would like to recognize the internal funding we have received over the past years from Mount Saint Vincent University for NCERW-related activities, which went a long way in supporting the work that has culminated in this collection.

Editor and Contributor Bios

MAYA EICHLER holds the Canada Research Chair in Social Innovation and Community Engagement and is an associate professor in political and Canadian studies and women's studies at Mount Saint Vincent University. She is also the director of the Centre for Social Innovation and Community Engagement in Military Affairs at Mount Saint Vincent University. Her current research focuses on gender and the armed forces, military sexual violence, military-to-civilian transitions, and community stories of war and peace. Eichler is the initiator of the Mount Network for Community-Engaged Research on War, and co-directs the international collaborative network Transforming Military Cultures.

REINA GREEN is an associate professor in the English Department at Mount Saint Vincent University where she teaches courses in early modern literature, including the drama of the period, and contemporary Canadian drama. Her research reflects the range of her teaching and focuses on performance and the actor-audience relationship. One of her recent projects has been on memorialization and performance. She has published in several book collections and academic journals.

TRACY MONIZ is an associate professor in the Department of Communication Studies at Mount Saint Vincent University. She teaches courses in writing, gender and media, and health communication. Her research has engaged with questions about gender ideology in news discourse, particularly in times of war. She is the editor of *Writing History: A Collection by New Writers,* volume 3 (Life Rattle Press 2013). More recently, she has explored the role of narrative and reflective writing in medical education.

CHAPTER 1: MILITARY VETERANS

LYNNE GOULIQUER is an associate professor of sociology at Laurentian University. Her research focuses on the sociology of institutions and marginalization theory as they apply to groups such as Canadian Armed Forces women, 2SLGBTQIA+ soldiers and their families, women firefighters, and Métis peoples.

KEN HOFFER is a veteran of the Royal Canadian Navy. He is a graduate of the Roméo Dallaire Institute's Veteran Trainers to Eradicate the Use of Child Soldiers program at Dalhousie University. Hoffer has deployed internationally to train military personnel, civilian police, and government officials in the prevention of recruitment and use of children as soldiers.

FRANK LETOURNEAU is a veteran of the Royal Canadian Navy and a victim of the Canadian government's LGBT Purge. After his forced resignation from the military, Letourneau remained in Halifax where he continues to reside.

JESSICA MILLER is a veteran of the Canadian Armed Forces and the founder of the Veteran Farm Project Society.

CARMEN POULIN is the associate dean of arts and a professor of psychology and gender and women's studies at the University of New Brunswick. Her research focuses on the impact of formal and informal social practices on women's and marginalized groups' daily lives.

JOHN WHELAN is a navy veteran, adjunct professor at Mount Saint Vincent University, and psychologist with over twenty-five years' experience working with serving and retired members of the military and RCMP.

DARL WOOD is a recently retired professor of women's studies, sociology, and interdisciplinary studies. After being purged from the military in 1978, she went on to become a feminist activist–advocate on the national and local stage.

CHAPTER 2: MILITARY FAMILIES

CATHERINE LITTLER is a PhD student at Dalhousie University, mother of two, and a military spouse. Her research primarily focuses on Canadian military spouses' experiences with food and how these experiences are gendered.

DEBORAH NORRIS is a professor in the Department of Family Studies and Gerontology at Mount Saint Vincent University. Informed by her background in family science, critical theories, and qualitative methodology, her research program focuses on military and veteran family research.

LEIGH SPANNER is a post-doctoral fellow at the Centre for Social Innovation and Community Engagement in Military Affairs at Mount Saint Vincent University. Her research involves feminist interrogations of state militaries, with a particular focus on military families.

CHAPTER 3: REFUGEE COMMUNITIES

VIYAN ALI is Kurdish from Kobani, Syria. She came to Halifax in 2016 with her family. Ali aspires to pursue a bachelor's degree in journalism and to then work as a journalist.

NAREEN HAJ ALI is Kurdish from Kobani, Syria. In her hometown, she worked as a lawyer. She moved to Halifax in 2016 with her husband and four children. Ali recently completed her studies in early childhood education at the Nova Scotia Community College.

CATHERINE BAILLIE ABIDI is a scholar–practitioner who bridges community and academia. She is a faculty member in the Department of Child and Youth Studies at Mount Saint Vincent University with twenty-five years of experience working in the humanitarian field, particularly in the areas of forced migration, peace and conflict, and refugee settlement.

AMARA BANGURA is a Sierra Leonean journalist based in Halifax with more than fifteen years of experience reporting and producing programs for international media organizations. He received the prestigious Gordon N. Fisher/JHR Journalism Fellowship at Massey College (University of Toronto).

MARIANELA FUERTES is an international human rights lawyer, former auxiliary judge of the Constitutional Court of Colombia, and a former restorative justice caseworker. Fuertes writes from the perspective of someone who was forcibly migrated due to political persecution.

CHAPTER 4: AFRICAN NOVA SCOTIAN COMMUNITIES

CLAUDINE BONNER is a scholar of African Canadian history and education and a member of the sociology department and women's and gender studies program at Acadia University. Her scholarship connects studies of Black Canada to the wider Atlantic World and crosses generational boundaries.

SUSAN M. BRIGHAM is a professor in the Faculty of Education at Mount Saint Vincent University. She is of African descent from an immigrant family. Her research interests include adult education, Africentricity, critical race theory, migration, and arts-informed research methodologies.

SYLVIA PARRIS-DRUMMOND, CEO of the Delmore "Buddy" Daye Learning Institute, is actively involved in a broad range of community organizations, including Akoma (AFC/Holdings), Feed Nova Scotia, and the Foundation for Black Communities.

CHAPTER 5: MILITARY HISTORIES ACROSS COMMUNITIES

KEN HYNES served over thirty years in the Canadian army (artillery), both at home and abroad. Hynes was the director of the First World War Centennial Exhibition Project (2014) and is currently the chief curator of the Army Museum Halifax Citadel.

DON JULIEN is a peacetime veteran of the Canadian Armed Forces, a Mi'kmaw historian and human rights activist, and the current executive director of the Confederacy of Mainland Mi'kmaq. Julien has received the Order of Canada and Order of Nova Scotia.

GREGORY KENNEDY is an associate professor of history and research director of the Acadian Studies Institute at the Université de Moncton. He is currently working on a book about the soldiers of the 165th (Acadian) Battalion during the First World War.

JENNA STEWART completed a combined major in political studies and history at Mount Saint Vincent University. She is proudly Mi'kmaq Acadian on her mother's side and Scottish English on her father's side.

CHAPTER 6: HALIFAX EXPLOSION

ROBERT BEAN, professor at NSCAD University, Halifax, is an artist, writer, and curator who has exhibited internationally and has published on photography, contemporary art, and cultural history.

JOHN DEWOLF is the principal of Narrative Environments Studio in Halifax, NS. He views program, story, and experience as integral to his interdisciplinary approach to design.

PAIGE FARAH is a social entrepreneur and founder of Progress in the Park and the community garden in Mulgrave Park, Halifax. In 2019, she was named a member of the Future City Builders youth cohort in Halifax, where she worked on a project addressing housing insecurity.

ANGELA HENDERSON (also a contributor to chapter 8) is a Canadian artist, designer, and educator who teaches at NSCAD University, Halifax. Her research focuses on experimental cartography, designing accessible cities, and collaboration with children in designing for unstructured play.

BARBARA LOUNDER is a visual artist and a founding member of Narratives in Space+Time Society. An experienced art educator, exhibiting artist, and writer, she has presented her work across Canada and internationally. Her current art practice focuses on walking as a creative methodology.

CATHERINE MARTIN is an Elder with the Millbrook Mi'kmaw community and an independent filmmaker, playwright, storyteller, and drummer. She held the Nancy's Chair in women's studies at Mount Saint Vincent University from 2015 to 2017, and is currently the director of Indigenous Community Engagement at Dalhousie University. In 2017, she was appointed to the Order of Canada, and in 2021, she received the Portia White Prize from Arts Nova Scotia.

JUANITA PETERS is a gifted and multi-award-winning storyteller, playwright, director, and actor, who worked in broadcast radio and television for many years. She is the executive director of the Africville Museum and has lectured at the Fountain School of Performing Arts at Dalhousie University.

CHAPTER 7: PEACE ACTIVISM

ROGER DAVIES has worked as a teacher and activist in Halifax since his arrival in Canada as a US Vietnam War resister over fifty years ago. He continues to be involved in community initiatives, such as Men for Change and refugee sponsorships.

BRIAN GIFFORD is the son of Giff Gifford, one of the founders of Veterans Against Nuclear Arms. Brian is active in the peace and environmental movements.

EL JONES is a poet, educator, journalist, and advocate. She was the fifth poet laureate of Halifax and the fifteenth Nancy's Chair in women's studies at Mount Saint Vincent University. She is an assistant professor in political and Canadian studies at Mount Saint Vincent University.

KATHRIN WINKLER is a teacher, artist, mother, grandmother, and member of the Nova Scotia Voice of Women. Principles of non-violence and non-harm fuel her interest in feminist peace activism.

CHAPTER 8: WAR AND ART

PETER DYKHUIS is an internationally exhibiting visual artist and critical writer. He was the director of the Anna Leonowens Gallery at NSCAD University from 1996 to 2007 and director/curator of the Dalhousie Art Gallery from 2007 to 2022.

WENDY ELLIOTT was a reporter and editor in Nova Scotia's Annapolis Valley for forty years. She has won a number of regional and national newspaper awards. Currently a columnist with the *Valley Journal Advertiser*, she is a Wolfville town council member.

ANDRIA HILL-LEHR is dedicated to telling the stories of women who are often ignored in popular historical narratives. She is author of *Mona Parsons: From Privilege to Prison, from Nova Scotia to Nazi Europe*, and her work has appeared in *Canada's History*, *Maclean's*, and *Saltscapes*.

JESSICA LYNN WIEBE is an interdisciplinary artist and military veteran whose work investigates the mechanisms of war, including the complex politics around gender, economy, the architecture of war, and the human condition. Most recently, her focus on the human condition has evolved as she develops work centred on the environment and the physical body through photography and video.

References

CHAPTER 1: MILITARY VETERANS

Kinsman, Gary, and Patrizia Gentile. *The Canadian War on Queers: National Security as Sexual Regulation*. Vancouver: University of British Columbia Press, 2010.

Thompson, Jim, and Wendy Lockhart. *Backgrounder for the Road to Civilian Life (R2CL) Program of Research into the Mental Health and Well-Being of Canadian Armed Forces Members/Veterans During Military-Civilian Transition*. Kingston: Canadian Institute for Military and Veteran Health Research, 2015. cimvhr.ca/documents/R2CL%20backgrounder%2029May2015_4_1.pdf.

Thompson, Kelly S. "We Are the Invisible: The Problem with How We Understand Our Veterans." *Globe and Mail*, November 8, 2019. theglobeandmail.com/opinion/article-we-are-the-invisible-the-problem-with-how-we-understand-our-veterans/.

Van Til, Linda, Jill Sweet, Alain Poirier, Kristofer McKinnon, Kerry Sudom, Sanela Dursun, and David Pedlar. *Life After Service Survey 2016: Executive Summary*. Charlottetown: Veterans Affairs Canada, 2017. veterans.gc.ca/eng/about-us/research-directorate/publications/reports/lass-2016.

CHAPTER 2: MILITARY FAMILIES

Canadian Forces Morale and Welfare Services (CFMWS). *Final Report: 2019 Military Family Resource Centre (MFRC) Governance Review*. Canadian Forces Morale and Welfare Services. Updated on March 19, 2019. cfmws.com/en/AboutUs/MFS/GovernanceandAccountability/Pages/Governance-Review-Working-Group.aspx.

Daigle, Pierre. *On the Homefront: Assessing the Well-Being of Canada's Military Families in the New Millennium*. Ottawa: Office of the Ombudsman, National Defence and Canadian Forces, 2013. ombudsman.forces.gc.ca/assets/OMBUDSMAN_Internet/docs/en/mf-fm-eng.pdf.

CHAPTER 3: REFUGEE COMMUNITIES

Baillie Abidi, Catherine. *Invisible Women, Concrete Barriers: Policy Roundtable on Issues Facing Refugee Women*. Halifax: Atlantic Centre of Excellence for Women's Health, Atlantic Council for International Cooperation, Atlantic Refugee and Immigrant Services Society, Canadian Red Cross, and Nova Scotia Advisory Council on the Status of Women, 2008.

Institute for Economics & Peace. *Global Peace Index 2019: Measuring Peace in a Complex World*. Sydney: Institute for Economics & Peace, 2020.

United Nations High Commissioner for Refugees. *Global Trends: Forced Displacement in 2020*. Geneva: UNHCR, 2021.

CHAPTER 4: AFRICAN NOVA SCOTIAN COMMUNITIES

Asante, Molefi Kete. *Afrocentricity: The Theory of Social Change*. Chicago: African American Images, 2003.

Battell Lowman, Emma, and Adam J. Barker. *Settler: Identity and Colonialism in 21st Century Canada*. Halifax: Fernwood Publishing, 2015.

Bernard, Delvina E., and Susan M. Brigham. *Theorizing Africentricity in Action: Who We Are Is What We See*. Halifax: Fernwood Publishing, 2012.

Blakeley, Phyllis Ruth. "William Hall, Canada's First Naval V.C.," *The Dalhousie Review* 37, no. 3 (1957): 250–58.

Brigham, Susan M. "Exploring the Connections Between Africentric Principles and Meditative Inquiry: Understanding Their Significance for Teaching and Learning in Adult Education Contexts." In *Engaging with Meditative Inquiry in Teaching, Learning, and Research: Realizing Transformative Potentials in Diverse Contexts*, edited by Ashwani Kumar, 31–46. New York: Routledge, 2022.

Brigham, Susan M. "Theorizing Race in Adult Education: Critical Race Theory." In *Building on Critical Traditions: Adult Education and Learning in Canada*, edited by Tom Nesbit, Susan M. Brigham, Nancy Taber, and Tara Gibb, 119–28. Toronto: Thompson Publishing, 2013.

Chilisa, Bagele. *Indigenous Research Methodologies*. Thousand Oaks: Sage Publishing, 2012.

Cooper, Afua. "A New Biography of the African Diaspora: The Life and Death of Marie-Joseph Angélique, Black Portuguese Slave Woman in New France, 1725-1734." In *Extending the Diaspora: New Histories of Black People*, edited by Dawne Y. Curry, Eric D. Duke, and Marshanda A. Smith, 46–76. Chicago: University of Illinois Press, 2009.

Cooper, Afua. *The Hanging of Angélique: The Untold Story of Canadian Slavery and the Burning of Old Montréal*. Athens: The University of Georgia Press, 2007.

Gilroy, Paul. *The Black Atlantic: Modernity and Double Consciousness*. Cambridge: Harvard University Press, 1993.

Hudson, Peter James, and Aaron Kamugisha. "On Black Canadian Thought." *The CLR James Journal* 20, nos. 1–2 (2014): 3–20.

Javed, Noor. "Afro vs. Afri." *Toronto Star*, February 2, 2008. thestar.com/news/2008/02/02/afro_vs_afri.html.

MacDonald, Bruce. "Pte. Joseph Alexander Parris – A No. 2 Construction Battalion Soldier's Story." *First World War Veterans of Guysborough County* (blog). January 30, 2014. guysboroughgreatwarveterans.blogspot.com/2014/01/pte-joseph-alexander-parris-no-2.html.

Mathieu, Sarah-Jane. *North of the Color Line: Migration and Black Resistance in Canada, 1870-1955*. Chapel Hill: University of North Carolina Press, 2010.

Pachai, Bridglal. "Hall, William (1829-1904)." In *Dictionary of Canadian Biography*, vol. 13. University of Toronto Press/Université Laval, 1994. Accessed on May 8, 2022. biographi.ca/en/bio/hall_william_1829_1904_13E.html.

Palmer, Colin. "Defining and Studying the Modern African Diaspora." *Perspectives on History: The Magazine of the American Historical Association* 36, no. 6 (September 1, 1998). historians.org/publications-and-directories/perspectives-on-history/september-1998/defining-and-studying-the-modern-african-diaspora.

Ruck, Calvin W. *Canada's Black Battalion: No. 2 Construction, 1916–1920.* Society for the Protection and Preservation of Black Culture in Nova Scotia, 1986.

Stewart, Anthony. *Visitor: My Life in Canada*. Halifax: Fernwood Publishing, 2014.

Walker, James W. St.G. "Race and Recruitment in World War I: Enlistment of Visible Minorities in the Canadian Expeditionary Force." *Canadian Historical Review* 70, no. 1 (1989): 1–26.

Whitfield, Harvey Amani. "Reviewing Blackness in Atlantic Canada and the African Atlantic Canadian Diaspora." *Acadiensis* 37, no. 2 (2008): 130–39.

Whitfield, Harvey Amani. *Blacks on the Border: The Black Refugees in British North America, 1815–1900.* Burlington: University of Vermont Press, 2006.

Winks, Robin W. *The Blacks in Canada: A History, Second Edition*. Montreal and Kingston: McGill-Queen's University Press, 2000.

CHAPTER 5: MILITARY HISTORIES ACROSS COMMUNITIES

Black, Dan. "The Chinese Labourers and the Secret Trains." *Toronto Star*, November 10, 2019a, A9.

Black, Dan. *Harry Livingstone's Forgotten Men: Canadians and the Chinese Labour Corps in the First World War*. Toronto: James Lorimer & Company, 2019.

Black, Dan, and John Boileau. *Old Enough to Fight: Canada's Boy Soldiers in the First World War.* Toronto: James Lorimer & Company, 2013.

Clarke, Nic. *Unwanted Warriors: Rejected Volunteers of the Canadian Expeditionary Force*. Vancouver: UBC Press, 2015.

Duguid, A. Fortesque. "Canadians in Battle, 1915–1918." *The Canadian Historical Association Report* 14, no. 1 (1935): 36–50.

Emery, J. C. Herbert, and Clint Levitt. "Cost of Living, Real Wages and Real Incomes in Thirteen Canadian Cities, 1900–1950." *Canadian Journal of Economics* 35, no. 1 (2002): 115–37.

Faragher, John Mack. *A Great and Noble Scheme: The Tragic Story of the Expulsion of the French Acadians from Their American Homeland*. Danvers, MA: W. W. Norton & Company, 2006.

Fowler, Wallace. *Checkmate*. N.p., Amazon.com Inc., 2016.

Gagnon, Jean-Pierre. *Le 22e bataillon (canadien-français) 1914–1919: Étude socio-militaire*. Quebec: Les Presses de l'Université Laval, 1986.

Kennedy, Gregory. "Answering the Call to Serve Their (Acadian) Nation: The Volunteers of the 165th Battalion, 1911–1917." *Histoire sociale/Social History* 51, no. 104 (2018): 279–99.

Léger, Claude. *Le Bataillon Acadien de la Première Guerre Mondiale*. N.p., 2001.

Library and Archives Canada. *Routine Orders*. 5th District (Jura), Canadian Forestry Corps, RG 9 III-B-3, vol. 3818-3819.

Morton, Desmond. *Fight or Pay: Soldiers' Families in the Great War*. Vancouver: UBC Press, 2004.

Morton, Desmond. *When Your Number's Up: The Canadian Soldier in the First World War*. Toronto: Random House of Canada, 1993.

Province of Nova Scotia. "Acadian Heartland: Records of the Deportation and Le Grand Dérangement, 1714-1768." Nova Scotia Archives, May 2020. archives.novascotia.ca/deportation/introduction/.

Teigrob, Robert. *Living with War: Twentieth-Century Conflict in Canadian & American History and Memory*. Toronto: University of Toronto Press, 2016.

Theobald, Andrew. *The Bitter Harvest of War: New Brunswick and the Conscription Crisis of 1917*. Fredericton: Goose Lane Editions, 2008.

Winegard, Timothy C. "'Now It Is All Over…I Am Practically No-Body': Indigenous Veterans of Canada and Australia and the Great War for Civilization." *First World War Studies* 10, no. 1 (2019): 12–30. doi:10.1080/19475020.2019.1701517.

CHAPTER 6: HALIFAX EXPLOSION

Armstrong, John Griffith. *The Halifax Explosion and the Royal Canadian Navy: Inquiry and Intrigue*. Vancouver: UBC Press, 2002.

Bean, Robert, Brian Lilley, Barbara Lounder, and Mary Elizabeth Luka. "Walking the Debris Field." Halifax: Narratives in Space+Time, 2017. Accessed on May 06, 2020. narrativesinspaceandtime.ca/projects/walking-the-debris-field/.

Cuthbertson, Ken. *The Halifax Explosion: Canada's Worst Disaster, December 6, 1917*. Toronto: HarperCollins Publishers, 2017.

Government of Canada. "Census of Canada, 1911." *Library and Archives Canada*, 2019. bac-lac.gc.ca/eng/census/1911/Pages/about-census.aspx.

Hébert, Michelle. *Enriched by Catastrophe: Social Work and Social Conflict After the Halifax Explosion*. Halifax: Fernwood, 2007.

IPCC (The Intergovernmental Panel on Climate Change) Working Group II. "Cross-Chapter Paper 6: Polar Regions." In *IPCC Sixth Assessment Report:* Climate Change 2022: Impacts, Adaptation and Vulnerability. IPCC, 2022. ipcc.ch/report/ar6/wg2/downloads/report/IPCC_AR6_WGII_CrossChapterPaper6.pdf.

Irving Shipbuilding Inc. "Irving Shipbuilding and Nunavut Research Institute Award $2 Million to Artic Research." Research and Social Impact. Irving Halifax Shipyard, October 4, 2016. Accessed on May 24, 2022. shipsforcanada.ca/our-stories/irving-shipbuilding-and-nunavut-research-institute-award-2-million-to-arctic-research-funding-awarded-to-nine-research-projects-across-canada.

Jones, Lindsay. "'Their Spirits Are Here': The Halifax Explosion's Untold Story of Mi'kmaw Communities Lost." *The Globe and Mail*, December 5, 2017. Accessed on May 06, 2020. theglobeandmail.com/news/national/halifax-explosion-anniversary-indigenous/article37194443/.

Kitz, Janet. *Shattered City: The Halifax Explosion and the Road to Recovery*. Halifax: Nimbus Publishing, 1989.

Kitz, Janet, and Joan Payzant. *December 1917: Re-Visiting the Halifax Explosion*. Halifax: Nimbus Publishing, 2015.

Knabb, Ken, ed. *Situationist International Anthology*. Translated by Ken Knabb. Berkeley: Bureau of Public Secrets, 1981.

Maybee, Janet. *Aftershock: The Halifax Explosion and the Persecution of Pilot Francis Mackey*. Halifax: Nimbus Publishing, 2015.

Meloney, Nic. "Mi'kmaw Playwright Recounts Family's Halifax Explosion Story from 'Nearly Forgotten' Turtle Grove." *CBC News*, December 6, 2017. Accessed on May 06, 2020. cbc.ca/news/indigenous/halifax-explosion-mikmaq-catherine-martin-1.4427386.

Morton, Suzanne. "Men and Women in a Halifax Working-Class Neighbourhood in the 1920s." PhD diss., Dalhousie University, 1990. Microfilm.

Province of Nova Scotia. "Halifax Explosion: A List of Those Who Died." *Nova Scotia Archives*. Accessed on May 13, 2022. novascotia.ca/archives/remembrance/.

Remes, Jacob A. C. *Disaster Citizenship: Survivors, Solidarity and Power in the Progressive Era*. Champaign: University of Illinois Press, 2016.

Ruffman, Alan, and Colin D. Howell, eds. *Ground Zero: A Reassessment of the 1917 Explosion in Halifax Harbour*. Halifax: Nimbus Publishing and Saint Mary's University, 1994.

Sutherland, David A, ed. *'We Harbour No Evil Design': Rehabilitation Efforts After the Halifax Explosion of 1917*. The Publications of the Champlain Society, vol. 78. Toronto: Champlain Society, 2017.

Zemel, Joel. *Scapegoat: The Extraordinary Proceedings Following the 1917 Halifax Explosion*. Halifax: New World Publishing, 2014.

CHAPTER 7: PEACE ACTIVISM

Ayed, Nahlah. "Killer Robots March into Uncharted Ethical Territory." *CBC Radio*. Updated on January 8, 2020. cbc.ca/radio/ideas/killer-robots-march-into-uncharted-ethical-territory-1.5289804.

Benjamin, Craig. "Veterans Against Veterans." *Cities: Halifax-Dartmouth Magazine* 2, no. 8 (January–February 1989): 19–21.

Bousquet, Tim. "Halifax Mayor Mike Savage Joins Mayors for Peace: International Organization Works for the Abolition of Nuclear Weapons." *The Coast* (January 30, 2014). thecoast.ca/RealityBites/archives/2014/01/30/halifax-mayor-mike-savage-joins-mayors-for-peace.

Brookfield, Tarah. *Cold War Comforts: Canadian Women, Child Safety, and Global Insecurity, 1945–1975.* Waterloo: Wilfrid Laurier University Press, 2012.

Clark, Joe. "Competitiveness and Security: Directions for Canada's International Relations." Ottawa: Ministry of Supply and Services Canada, 1985.

Cortright, David. "The Peace Movement Won the INF Treaty. We Must Fight to Preserve it." *The Nation* (November 14, 2018). thenation.com/article/archive/nuclear-arms-inf-treaty-peace-movement/.

Department of National Defence. *Challenge and Commitment: A Defence Policy for Canada.* Ottawa: Department of National Defence, 1987.

Devet, Robert. "Halifax Day of Peace: 'Hiroshima was a city so similar to Halifax that it is frightening.'" *The Nova Scotia Advocate,* August 6, 2020. nsadvocate.org/2020/08/06/halifax-day-of-peace-hiroshima-was-a-city-so-similar-to-halifax-that-it-is-frightening/.

Duckworth, Martin, dir. *Return to Dresden.* 1986. Montreal: National Film Board of Canada.

Dunlop, Malcolm. "Vets Talk Peace with Soviet Counterparts." *The Chronicle Herald,* May 26, 1987.

Early, Frances. "'A Grandly Subversive Time': The Halifax Branch of the Voice of Women in the 1960s." In *Mothers of the Municipality: Women, Work, and Social Policy in Post-1945 Halifax,* edited by Judith Fingard and Janet Guildford, 253–280. Toronto: University of Toronto Press, 2015.

Genesio, Jerry. "Giff Gifford." *Veterans for Peace, Inc.* 23 (Spring 1993): 1.

Gifford, C. G. "Pathfinder." In *This Was My War: A Collection of Memories of the 1939-1945 Conflict,* edited by Ian Maxwell. Tancook Island, NS: Little Daisy Press, 1992.

Hoare, Eva. "Forces' Nuclear Team Watching Submarine." *The Halifax Mail-Star*, September 29, 1986.

Kastner, Jill. "Standing on the Brink: The Secret War Scare of 1983." *The Nation*, May 31, 2018. thenation.com/article/archive/standing-on-the-brink-the-secret-war-scare-of-1983/.

Kramer, Andrew E., and Megan Specia. "What is the I.N.F. Treaty and Why Does it Matter?" *The New York Times*, February 1, 2019. nytimes.com/2019/02/01/world/europe/inf-treaty.html.

MacDonald, Sharon. "A Passionate Voice for Equality, Justice, and Peace: Nova Scotia's Mary Russell Chesley." In *Making Up the State: Women in 20th-Century Atlantic Canada*, edited by Janet Guildford and Suzanne Morton, 45–55. Acadiensis Press, 2010.

Mansour, Valerie. "An Old Soldier's Battle for Peace in a Military Town." *Atlantic Insight* 8, no. 2 (February 1986): 19–23.

Mayors for Peace. "About Us." Hiroshima Peace Culture Foundation. Accessed on May 16, 2022. mayorsforpeace.org/en/about-us/outline-m4p/.

Mayors for Peace. "Program to Promote Solidarity of Cities Towards the Total Abolition of Nuclear Weapons." Hiroshima Peace Culture Foundation. Accessed on May 28, 2022. mayorsforpeace.org/english/aboutus/promote.html.

Mills, Rob. "War Vet Following the Beat of Anti-Nuclear Drum." *Halifax Mail-Star*, September 14, 1989, C14.

McKenna, Brian, dir. *Death by Moonlight: Bomber Command*. 1991. Montreal: National Film Board of Canada.

NobelPrize.org. "The Nobel Peace Prize 1995." Nobel Prize Outreach AB, Accessed on May 15, 2022. nobelprize.org/prizes/peace/1995/summary/.

Nova Scotia Advisory Council on the Status of Women. *The Nova Scotia Nine: Remarkable Women, Then and Now*. Halifax: Province of Nova Scotia, 2014. women.novascotia.ca/sites/default/files/Publications/NS9_2021/NovaScotiaNine_full_WEB_2021.pdf.

Nova Scotia Voice of Women for Peace. "A Call for HRM to join the ICAN CITY APPEAL: Treaty on the Prohibition of Nuclear Weapons." Change.org. Accessed on June 18, 2022. change.org/p/mayor-mike-savage-and-hrm-council-a-call-for-hrm-to-join-the-icans-city-appeal-treaty-on-the-prohibition-of-nuclear-weapons.

Olds, Kathleen, and Julia-Simone Rutgers. "Emissions Footprint." *Ecology & Action* 36, no. 3 (Fall 2018): 2–3. ecologyaction.ca/sites/default/files/images-documents/Ecology%20&%20Action%20-%20Fall%20 2018%20-%20Online%203.pdf.

Pakula, Andrew, and Mark Pancer. "Interview with a Peacemaker-Veteran." *Peace Magazine* 1, no. 9 (December 1985): 17.

Peace Pledge Union. "Remembrance Briefing Notes." Peace Pledge Union. Accessed on May 16, 2022. ppu.org.uk/remembrance/remembrance-briefing-notes.

Pugwash Conferences on Science and World Affairs. Accessed on May 15, 2022. pugwash.org/.

Scott, Marian. "Vietnam War Resisters Were Welcomed as Heroes in Canada." *Montreal Gazette,* September 16, 2017. montrealgazette.com/news/local-news/for-vietnam-war-resisters-moving-to-canada-was-the-best-thing-they-ever-did.

Senate of Canada. Senators' Statements: The Late Muriel Duckworth, C.M." *Debates of the Senate*. September 17, 2009. Ottawa: Senate of Canada. publications.gc.ca/collections/collection_2017/sen/Y3-402-53-eng.pdf.

Squires, Jessica. *Building Sanctuary: The Movement to Support Vietnam War Resisters in Canada, 1965-73*. Vancouver: UBC Press, 2013.

Teigrob, Robert. *Living with War: Twentieth-Century Conflict in Canadian and American History and Memory*. Toronto: University of Toronto Press, 2016.

Wilt, James. "Canada Still Doesn't Know How Much Pollution Its Military Emits." *Vice,* March 13, 2017. vice.com/en_ca/article/ypknzj/canada-still-doesnt-know-how-much-pollution-its-military-emits.

CHAPTER 8: WAR AND ART

Berry, Steve. "Statue Honouring Nova Scotia Woman, Who Hid Allied Airman from Nazis, Unveiled." *CBC News*. CBC/Radio Canada, May 6, 2017. Accessed on May 27, 2022. cbc.ca/news/canada/nova-scotia/mona-parsons-statue-unveiled-1.4102941#:~:text=The%20joy%20is%20almost%20too,make%20the%20sculpture%20a%20reality.

Elliott, Robbins. Letter, 21 April 1945, Robbins Elliott fonds, Esther Clark Wright Archives, Acadia University, Wolfville, 2013.

Elliott, Wendy. "A Long Road to Recognition for This War Hero." *This Week* (blog). February 10, 2018. Accessed on May 37, 2022. lowerduck.blogspot.com/2018/02/a-long-road-to-recognition-for-this-war.html. com/2018/02/a-long-road-to-recognition-for-this-war.html.

Elliott, Wendy. "Wolfville Vigil Will Continue." *The Kentville Advertiser*. October 11, 2011.

Hill-Lehr, Andria. *Mona Parsons: From Privilege to Prison, From Nova Scotia to Nazi Europe*. Halifax: Nimbus Publishing, 2017.

Kosters, Elizabeth. "Why Mona." Unpublished Presentation to Wolfville Town Council, 2015.

Reeves, Joshua. "Suspended Identification: *Atopos* and the Work of Public Memory." *Philosophy and Rhetoric* 46, no. 3 (July 2013): 306–27. doi:101353/par.2013.0029.

Virilio, Paul, and Sylvère Lotringer. *Pure War*. Translated by Mark Polizzotti and Brian O'Keeffe. Los Angeles: Semiotext(e)/Foreign Agents, 1983.

Wright, Esther Clark. *Blomidon Rose*. Whitby, ON: Ryerson Press, 1957.

Young, James E. "The Counter-monument: Memory Against Itself in Germany Today." *Critical Inquiry* 18, no. 2 (Winter 1992): 267–96. jstor.org/stable/1343784.

CONCLUSION

Barthes, Ronald. *Image, Music, Text*. Selected and translated by Stephen Heath. London: Fontana Press, 1977.

Pictou, Sherry Mae. "Decolonizing Mi'kmaw Memory of Treaty: L'sɨtkuk's Learning with Allies in Struggle for Food and Lifeways." PhD diss., Dalhousie University, 2017.

Index

Page numbers in italics refer to figures.